GOD'S

FINAL

J
U
B
I
L
E
E

Evangelist Dan Goodwin

Evangelist Dan Goodwin
80 Huff LN
Reynolds Station, KY 42368

www.heavenboundone.net

dgoodwin@uplink.net

ISBN: 978-1-60208-340-0

1st Print February 2014
2nd Reprint March 2014
3rd Reprint with revisions April 2014
4th Reprint with revisions May 2014

All Scriptures from the 1611 King James Bible

Printed in the United States of America by
Faith Baptist Church Publications
Fort Pierce, FL 34982
www.fbcpublications

2

FOREWORD

This book by Brother Dan Goodwin is about Christians in these last days being spiritually prepared for the return of Jesus Christ from Heaven. It has been my experience in attending churches and speaking with pastors that the subject is never addressed because they consider Biblical prophecy a distraction.

However, Jesus said after answering the disciples question about signs of His coming again, "...*when ye shall see all these things, know that it is near, even at the doors*" (Mt.24:33).

Time and space will not permit a detailed examination of the many "things" that Jesus said the world would be like and specific moral, national, and international events that would occur as signs of His soon return. This is why you will want to read this book.

Just a few of the important prophetic headlines that have come to my desk the same day I write this forward are:

170,000 rockets are aimed at Israel
Hillary endorses same-sex marriage
Thief arrested with drone's help
Obama picks Muslim as CIA Chief
Germans o.k. microchip implant
TBN dropping prophecy programs
100,000 Christians die for their faith each year
Jesus' picture now unconstitutional

Jesus also said it would be like the days of Sodom when He would come again (Luke 17:30). Oklahoma passed a law with 70% majority that marriage consisted of one man and one woman. A federal judge ruled the Oklahoma law unconstitutional. Homosexual marriages are now as common as the once traditional marriage.

Chapters 4 through 19 present in detail world conditions

3

and events that would occur during the seven years preceding the return of Jesus Christ. In Revelation Chapter 8, verse 9, it is prophesied that just before Christ returns that one-third of the creatures in the sea will die. The prophecy does not indicate this would happen in all seas or oceans, or in just one sea or ocean. Nevertheless, the first week of February 2014, the nuclear waste from the three nuclear generators that were damaged two years ago finally reached the West Coast from California to British Columbia. Entire species of fish life like sardines and star fish were practically destroyed. Fishermen in the area cannot fish and those living on the West Coast cannot eat the fish sold at the market. Many have gotten sick and some have even died.

I present all the preceding as an example of the prophecies being fulfilled that are to immediately precede the coming of Jesus Christ.

How are you to be prepared for the Lord's coming? How are you to witness to your family and friends? A very effective way to do this would be to give them a copy of this book. Each of us has a responsibility to let the unsaved and the sleeping church members know that Jesus said, *"But ye, brethren, are not in darkness, that that day should overtake you as a thief"* (I Th. 5:4).

Rev. Noah W. Hutchings
Southwest Radio Ministries
P.O. Box 100
Bethany, OK 73008

TABLE OF CONTENTS

The surest fact in the world is not death,
but the return of the Lord Jesus Christ!
M. R. DeHaan (1947)

5

DEDICATION

This book is dedicated to my good friend Herb Kinman who went to be with the Lord on Sunday, February 16, 2014, just a few days before this book went to the publishers. Brother Herb lived a busy life in Carrollton, KY. He was a Father, Grandfather, and the owner of a GM Dealership. He was also a preacher and counselor to many. Brother Herb needed someone on the outside he could "unload on" from time to time. I believe I was that person (or at least one of them) in his life. We often spoke on the phone for over an hour, usually late at night. We prayed together about many things. I have heard just about every one of his stories he had told of his past at least three times! (But I always laughed anyway) Brother Herb was a great supporter of my ministry. He was very excited about this book and was looking forward to getting a copy. I suspect that since he is now walking the streets of gold, he no longer has need of it. He is now seeing first-hand the preparations being made in Heaven for a wedding and for the sounding of the trumpet! One of the last text messages I received from Brother Herb just before he left this world was "I love the cover of that new book!".

I have wept at the loss of my good friend and miss him very much. The timing of his passing to Glory makes the publishing of this book bittersweet, but I am comforted with the knowledge that I will be seeing my good friend again soon. And when I get to Heaven, I will not be surprised to find he has been selling chariots to the saints there!

INTRODUCTION

The book you are holding in your hands was written to sound an alarm to the people of God. Jesus is coming, and He is coming soon! We do not know the exact day or hour of His coming, but it is soon. When we read the Scriptures, we see that at the end of each age, God always raised up a few men to sound the horn for the next generation. Noah sounded the horn before the floods came. Jeremiah and Ezekiel sounded the horn concerning the seventy-year captivity to come. Daniel sounded the horn at the end of the seventy years, and John the Baptist was brought on the scene as the forerunner to bring in the New Testament Age and point people to Christ. After the rapture, God will send His two witnesses to sound the horn for the Jews during the Tribulation. After considering all this, do you think God would end the Church Age without someone to sound the horn? Not on your life! It is my prayer that God will use this book to warn this lukewarm generation of His soon coming! I pray that the truths in this book will stir people across our land to once again look for the soon return of Jesus Christ.

Just as the world is changing around us, the church too is changing. Bible Prophecy was once an exciting topic of preaching in our pulpits. Now it is the subject of critics and scoffers. I believe God intended for us to be concerned with the future. The Bible is a futuristic book. Basically, prophecy is the future. Prophecy is history written in advance; it is His-story pre-written. Even though many will say they are not concerned with future events, the opposite is true. There are around seven billion people on the earth today. Nearly every one of them is living for the future. Most of us will check the weather to see what we need to wear tomorrow. Young people are looking forward to getting out of high school. College folks look forward to getting their careers started. Young adults look forward to marriage. People at their jobs look forward to a promotion. Older folks look forward to retirement. We plan investments for the future. All of us to some degree are living for the future! The same preachers who criticize prophecy, do not seem to have a problem setting a date to go golfing in THE FUTURE!

WHY THIS BOOK:

The most important and exciting part of a race is the finish. When a runner gets to the last lap he seems to find strength within himself to push a little harder and to give one final effort to win. I believe we are near the end; I believe we are on the final lap of this age. The finish line is just around the next bend. It is not time to be lazy; it is not time to lag behind. It is time to pull out all the stops and run harder and faster than we ever have before! Let's not be the generation that quit at the last lap; let's be the generation that crossed the finish line in a blaze of glory! Let's go out with a bang! Let's do it for souls, let's do it for our churches; let's do it for the glory of God!

He which testifieth these things saith, Surely I come quickly. Amen. Even so, come, Lord Jesus.
Revelation 22:20

TEN PROOFS OF A PRE-TRIBULATION RAPTURE
Chapter 1

Before we get started on our prophetic journey, it is vitally important that we settle this matter of a pre-tribulation rapture. After much study it is my belief that Jesus Christ is coming back the second time in two stages just as He came the first time in two stages. Two thousand years ago Jesus was born in a stable in Bethlehem. It was a secret revealed only to a select few: Zacharias and Elizabeth, Joseph and Mary, Simeon and Anna, and a few shepherds. Later, some thirty years later, He was baptized of John in the Jordan, and began His 3 ½ year ministry. Later, He rode into Jerusalem on the donkey and presented Himself to Israel on Palm Sunday. He was crucified four days later on Passover just as it was prophesied. This second stage was not a secret, but it was in fact prophesied in the Scriptures that Messiah would ride into Jerusalem on that exact day!

So, we have established that the first coming of Christ was in two stages. The second coming of Christ is also in two stages. He comes secretly at what we call the rapture, to snatch away His bride. Seven years later, after Daniel's 70th week (The 7 year Tribulation) is fulfilled; He comes back to the earth with us. He will put down the Antichrist at the battle of Armageddon and will set up His kingdom. Most people missed the first coming of Christ, and I am afraid most are not looking for Him today. Truly history does repeat itself. Jesus Himself said it would be this way.

Lu 18:8 "...Nevertheless when the Son of man cometh, shall he find faith on the earth?"

The word "rapture" is not in the Bible. However, we get the word from the phrase "caught up" in the following passage:

1Thessalonians 4:13-18 But I would not have you to be ignorant, brethren, concerning them which are asleep, that ye sorrow not, even as others which have no hope. For if we believe that Jesus died and rose again, even so them also which sleep in Jesus will God bring with him. For this we say unto you by the word of the Lord, that we which are alive and remain unto the coming of the Lord shall not prevent them which are asleep. For the Lord himself shall descend from heaven with a shout, with the voice of the archangel, and with the trump of God: and the dead in Christ shall rise first: Then we which are alive and remain shall be <u>caught up</u> together with them in the clouds, to meet the Lord in the air: and so shall we ever be with the Lord. Wherefore comfort one another with these words.

Another Bible term for the word "rapture" is the word "translated" from the story of Enoch in the Old Testament as given in the book of Hebrews.
Hebrews 11:5 By faith Enoch was <u>translated</u> that he should not see death; and was not found, because God had translated him: for before his translation he had this testimony, that he pleased God.
Since the word "rapture" is so widely understood today, it is the term we shall use in this book. Some other passages for the rapture are: I Corinthians 15:51-56
Behold, I shew you a mystery; We shall not all sleep, but we shall all be changed, In a moment, in the twinkling of an eye<u>, at the last trump:</u> for the <u>trumpet shall sound</u>, and the dead shall be raised incorruptible, and we shall be changed. For this corruptible must put on incorruption, and this mortal must put on immortality. So

when this corruptible shall have put on incorruption, and this mortal shall have put on immortality, then shall be brought to pass the saying that is written, Death is swallowed up in victory. O death, where is thy sting? O grave, where is thy victory? The sting of death is sin; and the strength of sin is the law.

John 14:1-4 Let not your heart be troubled: ye believe in God, believe also in me. In my Father's house are many mansions: if it were not so, I would have told you. I go to prepare a place for you. And if I go and prepare a place for you, <u>I will come again, and receive</u> you unto myself; that where I am, there ye may be also. And whither I go ye know, and the way ye know.

Re 4:1 After this I looked, and, behold, a door was opened in heaven: and the first voice which I heard was as it were of <u>a trumpet</u> talking with me; which said<u>, Come up hither,</u> and I will shew thee things which must be hereafter.

The rapture is not a new teaching as is claimed by some, but has been taught for centuries. Here are some quotes from time past:

"I will add this more, namely, what may be conceived to be the cause of this **RAPTURE** of the saints on high to meet the Lord in the clouds, rather than to wait his coming to earth....What if it be, that they may be PRESERVED during the Conflagration of the earth and the works thereof, 2 Pet.3:10, that as Noah and his family were preserved from the Deluge by being lift up above the waters in the Ark; so should the saints at the Conflagration be lift up in the clouds unto their Ark, Christ, to be preserved there from the deluge of fire, wherein the wicked shall be consumed?" ("The Works of Joseph Mede," 1672, London edition, Book IV, p.776)

"**And therefore, when in the end the Church shall be suddenly caught up from this**, it is said, "There shall be tribulation such as has not been since the beginning, neither shall be."(2) For this is the last contest of the righteous, in which, when they overcome they are crowned with incorruption." Irenaeus in his book "Against Heresies" 130-202 A.D. An eyewitness to the Apostle John and a disciple of Polycarp.

11

"We who see that terrible things have begun, and know that still more terrible things are imminent, may regard it as the greatest advantage to depart from it as quickly as possible. Do you not give God thanks, do you not congratulate yourself, **that by an early departure you are taken away, and delivered from the shipwrecks and disasters that are imminent?**"
From the "Treatise of Cyprian" (200 AD – 258 AD)

For all the saints and elect of God are gathered, prior to the tribulation that is to come, and are taken to the Lord lest they see the confusion that is to overwhelm the world because of our sins.
Ephraim the Syrian In his work, "*On The Last Times 2*" (306 AD – 373 AD)

There are basically three views concerning when the rapture will occur. The pre-tribulation view is that the rapture occurs before the Tribulation. The mid-tribulation view is that the rapture occurs at the middle of the seven years, and the post-tribulation view is that the rapture occurs at the end and that all believers will go through the terrible Tribulation. We shall not take the time debating the errors of the latter two. I will say that many believers today have grown tired of waiting and have changed their position on the timing of the rapture. I tell you here and now without apology that I have not changed my mind concerning the rapture. **Let me give you ten irrefutable reasons why I believe the rapture comes before the seven-year Tribulation:**

1. Because the rapture is imminent.

In other words, it could happen any moment! It means that God has not told us the specific day or hour of His return. If the rapture were to happen at the middle or at the end, it would be easy to pinpoint the rapture to the very day and would not be a surprise, thus it would not be imminent.

The Bible proposes the rapture is a day no man can know while Christ's second coming is a day foretold right to the very day. Matthew 25:13 says Jesus will come at a time no man can know, while Revelation 12:6 specifies the coming of Christ exactly 1,260 days after the breaking of the peace treaty.

Matthew 25:13 Watch therefore, for ye know neither the day nor the hour wherein the Son of man cometh.

Revelation 12:6 And the woman fled into the wilderness, where she hath a place prepared of God, that they should feed her there a thousand two hundred and threescore days.

The 1,260 days begin when the Antichrist enters the Temple and declares himself to be God. (Matt. 24:15-21, 2 Thess. 2:4) This event will take place at the middle of the seven-year Tribulation (Dan 9:27).

See the following Scriptures:

Luke 12:40 Be ye therefore ready also: for the Son of man cometh at an hour when ye think not.

Matthew 24:36 But of that day and hour knoweth no man, no, not the angels of heaven, but my Father only.

Matthew 25:13 Watch therefore, for ye know neither the day nor the hour wherein the Son of man cometh.

2. Because the rapture is the "blessed hope."

Titus 2:13 Looking for that blessed hope, and the glorious appearing of the great God and our Saviour Jesus Christ;

What is blessed is that Christ comes and delivers us from the Tribulation to come upon the world. It would not be considered the "blessed hope" at the middle or at the end of the Tribulation. Praise the Lord He will "catch His bride away" BEFORE the trouble starts.

3. Because the Lord has not appointed us to wrath.

The Tribulation is the wrath of God upon this world as well as God dealing with Israel. God has not appointed the saved to wrath. Do not confuse chastisement and persecution that believers go through with God's wrath, they are two separate things entirely.

1Thessalonians 5:9 For God hath not appointed us to wrath, but

to obtain salvation by our Lord Jesus Christ,
Romans 8:1 There is therefore now no condemnation to them
which are in Christ Jesus, who walk not after the flesh, but after
the Spirit.
John 5:24 Verily, verily, I say unto you, He that heareth my word,
and believeth on him that sent me, hath everlasting life, and shall
not come into condemnation; but is passed from death unto life.
Revelation 3:10 Because thou hast kept the word of my patience, I
also will keep thee from the hour of temptation, which shall come
upon all the world, to try them that dwell upon the earth.

Daniel 9:24-27 teaches that the Tribulation is the 70th week of years of judgment for Israel and has nothing to do with the church age. This will be dealt with in another chapter.

4. Because there is no mention of the church after Revelation Chapter 4.

The seven churches are mentioned in Revelation Chapters 2 and 3. The rapture takes place followed by the seven years of the Tribulation. Revelation 4:1 *After this I looked, and, behold, a door was opened in heaven: and the first voice which I heard was as it were of a trumpet talking with me; which said, Come up hither, and I will shew thee things which must be hereafter.*

The reason the church is not mentioned again until the end of Revelation is because all believers have been taken out at the rapture. The true church is gone. God is once again dealing with the Jews in the 70th week mentioned in Daniel 9:27. The Tribulation is the final week (seven years) of the Old Testament. The entire Church Age is grafted in between Daniel's 69th & 70th week.

Again, we will look more at Daniel 9 in another chapter so if you do not grasp what I mean by these 70 weeks, do not despair. It is explained later in great detail.

5. Because of the removal of the Restrainer, The Holy Spirit of God, who indwells all believers.

I think all of us agree that the Antichrist comes on the scene as the first horseman at the BEGINNING of the seven-year Tribulation.

Revelation 6:1-2 And I saw when the Lamb opened one of the seals, and I heard, as it were the noise of thunder, one of the four beasts saying, Come and see. And I saw, and behold a white horse: and he that sat on him had a bow; and a crown was given unto him: and he went forth conquering, and to conquer.

This white horse carries the Antichrist into the position of a one-world dictator at the opening of the very first of the seven seals. This scene is at the beginning of the seven-year Tribulation. (Do not confuse him with Jesus who comes on a white horse in Revelation 19:11 at the end of the Tribulation.) Satan is the great counterfeiter. He has a counterfeit of everything God has. He has counterfeit Bibles, counterfeit churches, and a counterfeit Spirit. Here we see that Antichrist is the counterfeit Messiah. He comes on a white horse just as Jesus will seven years later.

What I want to show you from our passage in 2Thessalonians is that this Antichrist, this man of sin, does not show up until after the Restrainer that indwells all believers is taken away. It is vital that you see this! Paul makes this perfectly clear in our passage.

1 Now we beseech you, brethren, by the coming of our Lord Jesus Christ, and by our gathering together unto him,
2 That ye be not soon shaken in mind, or be troubled, neither by spirit, nor by word, nor by letter as from us, as that the day of Christ is at hand.
3 Let no man deceive you by any means: for that day shall not come, except there come a falling away first, and that man of sin be revealed, the son of perdition;

15

4 Who opposeth and exalteth himself above all that is called
God, or that is worshipped; so that he as God sitteth in the
temple of God, shewing himself that he is God.
5 Remember ye not, that, when I was yet with you, I told you
these things?
6 And now ye know what withholdeth that he might be
revealed in his time.
7 For the mystery of iniquity doth already work: only he
who now letteth will let, until he be taken out of the way.
8 And then shall that Wicked be revealed, whom the Lord
shall consume with the spirit of his mouth, and shall destroy
with the brightness of his coming: 2 Thessalonians 2:1-8

Notice in verse 2 that "the day of Christ" is the second
coming of Christ at the end of the seven-year Tribulation.
When you get the context of the passage by going back to 2
Thessalonians 1:7-12, it is obvious that the "day of Christ" in
2 Thessalonians 2:2 is speaking of the second coming at the
end of the Tribulation.
2 Thessalonians 1:7-12 And to you who are troubled rest
with us, when the Lord Jesus shall be revealed from heaven
with his mighty angels, In flaming fire taking vengeance on
them that know not God, and that obey not the gospel of our
Lord Jesus Christ: Who shall be punished with everlasting
destruction from the presence of the Lord, and from the glory
of his power; When he shall come to be glorified in his
saints, and to be admired in all them that believe (because
our testimony among you was believed) in that day.
Wherefore also we pray always for you, that our God would
count you worthy of this calling, and fulfil all the good
pleasure of his goodness, and the work of faith with power:
That the name of our Lord Jesus Christ may be glorified in
you, and ye in him, according to the grace of our God and
the Lord Jesus Christ.
Scripture clearly teaches that the Saints are removed at the

rapture as seen here:

Revelation 4:1 After this I looked, and, behold, a door was opened in heaven: and the first voice which I heard was as it were of a trumpet talking with me; which said, Come up hither, and I will shew thee things which must be hereafter.

Revelation Chapters 4 and 5 show what takes place in Heaven immediately after the rapture. Revelation 6 is the start of the seven-year Tribulation (Daniel's 70th week) with the opening of the first seal which introduces the Antichrist coming on the scene: *(Revelation 6:1-2) And I saw when the Lamb opened one of the seals, and I heard, as it were the noise of thunder, one of the four beasts saying, Come and see. And I saw, and behold a <u>white horse: and he that sat on him</u> had a bow; and a crown was given unto him: and he went forth conquering, and to conquer.*

With the clear teaching of the arrival of the Antichrist at the first seal in Revelation 6, which is at the beginning of the Tribulation, let's go back to 2 Thessalonians 2:1-8 and show proof that <u>no believers will be here when the first seal is opened.</u> This passage clearly teaches that the Holy Spirit which is the "restrainer" that indwells all believers, will be removed before the Antichrist comes on the scene. *And now ye know what <u>withholdeth</u> that he might be revealed in his time. For the mystery of iniquity doth already work: <u>only he who now letteth will let, until he be taken out of the way.</u> And then shall that Wicked be revealed, whom the Lord shall consume with the spirit of his mouth, and shall destroy with the brightness of his coming: 2 Thessalonians 2:6-8*

"What withholdth" is the Holy Spirit of God who indwells all believers. He restrains (letteth) the work of Satan until He is "taken out of the way" at the rapture. Therefore, there can not be any doubt about the rapture being BEFORE the Tribulation. The Holy Spirit cannot leave without us, my friend! He indwells all believers. This passage teaches that all believers along with the Holy Spirit's influence and restraining power will be removed right before the Antichrist is revealed. All the "salt and light" will be gone. That is the rapture folks!

It is plain that the Scriptures teach a pre-tribulation rapture. Do not be fooled by all the confusion and change that many of today's "preachers" are giving us. The Bible has not changed! Truth never changes.

Before we move on, let me give just a little more insight into this important passage of Scripture. It is so vital that we get a solid grasp of these truths.

There are actually three distinct things spoken of in 2 Thessalonians 2:1-8 that must happen before the second coming of Christ (called the day of Christ in 2 Thessalonians 2:2) can occur. The church in Thessalonica had been deceived into thinking that the second coming, the return of Jesus at the end of the seven years, was at hand. Paul was writing to clear up this controversy. He says in verse 3, "Let no man deceive you…" and gives them three reasons why THE DAY OF CHRIST (second coming at end of the Tribulation) is not at hand.

A. The "falling away" must come first.

There are two schools of thought as to what the "falling away" is. Some say it is in fact the rapture. I used to believe this. After much prayer and study, I no longer hold to this view. Nowhere else in Scripture is "falling" used to denote the rapture. In fact, "falling" is seldom ever used in reference to something good. There is no other place in the Bible where this phrase is used, but I did find these two Scriptures that use the phrase "fall away."

Luke 8:13 They on the rock are they, which, when they hear, receive the word with joy; and these have no root, which for a while believe, and in time of temptation fall away.

Hebrews 6:6 If they shall fall away, to renew them again unto repentance; seeing they crucify to themselves the Son of God afresh, and put him to an open shame.

Would you agree that the phrase "fall away" is just another tense of the phrase "falling away?" And would you agree that both of these passages use it in a negative context? A good friend and missionary in Romania, Peter Heisey, made this observation concerning Luke 8:13. They "fell away" because they "had no root." Wow, that really sheds some light on our passage does it not? I believe the "falling away" mentioned in our passage is speaking about a departing from the faith in the lives of the saints as well as the church. This has been happening for centuries, but you must admit that in the last few decades we have been on a slippery downward slope. The Bible plainly says that things will get worse and worse in the last days.

This know also, that in the last days perilous times shall come. For men shall be lovers of their own selves, covetous, boasters, proud, blasphemers, disobedient to parents, unthankful, unholy, Without natural affection, trucebreakers, false accusers, incontinent, fierce, despisers of those that are good, Traitors, heady, highminded, lovers of pleasures more than lovers of God; Having a form of godliness, but denying the power thereof: from such turn away. (2 Timothy 3:1-5)

Is this not a description of "falling away?" If you understand the prophetic lessons of the seven churches in Revelation Chapters 2 and 3, then you must see that we are living in the Laodicean age and that our churches today fit the sad description given of her in this passage: *And unto the angel of the church of the Laodiceans write; These things saith the Amen, the faithful and true witness, the beginning of the creation of God; I know thy works, that thou art neither cold nor hot: I would thou wert cold or hot. So then because thou art lukewarm, and neither cold nor hot, I will spue thee out of my mouth. Because thou sayest, I am rich, and increased with goods, and have need of nothing; and knowest not that thou art wretched,*

19

and miserable, and poor, and blind, and naked: I counsel thee to buy of me gold tried in the fire, that thou mayest be rich; and white raiment, that thou mayest be clothed, and that the shame of thy nakedness do not appear; and anoint thine eyes with eyesalve, that thou mayest see. (Revelation 3:14-18)

I said there are three specific things Paul mentioned that must take place before the "Day of Christ."

A. The "falling away" must come first.

B. The Restrainer (Holy Spirit) must be removed.

Friends, there is only one thing holding the Antichrist back. That one thing is Spirit-filled believers! I believe the Holy Spirit does His work through us. I believe it is the influence of God's Spirit in the assembly of believers around the world that holds back Satan's one-world plan. I believe that Satan has had a man ready to be his Antichrist in every generation. I believe Hitler was Satan's hand picked man. However, it was not the time. I believe Satan has a man prepared right now to step on the scene. Only one thing is holding this man back and that is Spirit-filled believers! When we are gone, when the trumpet sounds, Antichrist will be revealed.

C. The Antichrist comes on the scene and is a world dictator for seven years.

These three things must come to pass before Christ can come on His white horse and set up the kingdom.

Revelation 19:11 *And I saw heaven opened, and behold a white horse; and he that sat upon him was called Faithful and True, and in righteousness he doth judge and make war.*

This is the TRUE Messiah. Antichrist is the false Messiah. Be sure you are following the right one.

Note: As America gets further from God, and as God's people become more like the world, we see less restraining power of God and more demonic activity. Imagine a whole world with no Christians and no Holy Spirit restraint! America is getting more wicked every day. Just take a moment and think of all the demonic television programs that we now

20

allow into our homes. I am talking about God's people, not the lost. I believe America has become evil because the church has lost its savour. God's people have "fallen away"; we have very little influence on the world around us anymore.

6. Because of the Old Testament types of the rapture.

1) Enoch was removed from God's wrath BEFORE the floods came.

2) Lot was delivered from Sodom BEFORE the fire fell.

3) Noah was lifted up above the floodwaters.

7. Because of the twenty-four Elders in the book of Revelation.

From Revelation 4:4 to 19:4 they are mentioned 12 times. I believe these "Elders" represent all believers in Heaven after the rapture. Just look at the characteristics of these Elders and it is plain to see: The crowns they cast at His feet, their praise of God, their clothing, etc. As soon as the trumpet sounds in Chapter 4:1, all believers are assembled in Heaven represented by the twenty-four Elders.

8. Because of the contrast between the rapture and the second coming.

The two simply can NOT be at the same time, or be the same event. See just a few examples here:

Rapture	**2nd Coming**
Coming for us John 14:1-4	Coming with us Rev. 19:14,
1 Thess. 4:14-17	Jude 1:14
As a thief in the night	Every eye shall see Him
1 Thess. 5:2	Rev. 1:7
Meets us in the clouds	Coming on a white horse
1 Thess. 4:16-17	Rev. 19:11
Imminent 1 Thess. 5:4-6	At end of 7 years
Luke 12:40	2 Thess. 2:3-8

9. The Church can not be overcome by Satan, but the Tribulation saints will be.

Matthew 16:18 *And I say also unto thee, That thou art Peter, and upon this rock I will build my church; and the gates of hell shall not prevail against it.*

Revelation 13:7 *And it was given unto him to make war with the saints, and to overcome them: and power was given him over all kindreds, and tongues, and nations.*
    If the saints in Revelation 13 can be overcome by Satan, they are not the church.

10. The many figures and types throughout the New Testament that are prophetic of a pre-tribulation rapture.

I will be dealing with these in later chapters so I will not go into detail here, but the Bible is filled with types and figures that prove a pre-tribulation rapture.
    The next great event on God's prophetic calendar is the rapture.
    Someone came up with a nice acrostic I want to share with you:
P- Placement of the church in Revelation
R- Removal of restraining power
E- Exempt from God's wrath
T- Twenty-four Elders
R- Rapture contrasted with Second Coming
I- Imminent return of Christ
B- Blessed hope

A WEDDING IN THE CLOUDS
Chapter 2

Revelation 21:2 And I John saw the holy city, new Jerusalem, coming down from God out of heaven, prepared as a bride adorned for her husband.

Revelation 21:9 And there came unto me one of the seven angels which had the seven vials full of the seven last plagues, and talked with me, saying, Come hither, I will shew thee the bride, the Lamb's wife.

There are many truths in the word of God that we seem to miss because we do not understand the Jewish customs of Israel. The customs that Israel practiced in Bible days, whether they fully understood them or not, actually coincided with Scripture and often pointed to Christ. Many of the parables and stories Jesus gave are not fully understood by us today because we lack an understanding of the Jewish customs. Many of the parables and truths that Jesus taught were intertwined around these Jewish customs. Did you know the customs that revolve around the Jewish wedding are based upon Biblical truths concerning Christ coming in the rapture to claim His bride?

In the previous chapter we settled the matter of a pre-tribulation rapture. In this chapter we are going to see the pre-tribulation rapture unfold before our very eyes as we look at the beautiful and prophetic Jewish customs of how a young man chose his bride.

In the text above, we see that all believers are one day going to be the bride of Christ. One day soon, when He comes for us at the rapture, for the first time ever, all believers will be a church assembled together in perfect unity

23

without spot or blemish and will become the bride of Christ.

Let's look at the Jewish practice of betrothal and marriage and see how it typifies Christ coming for His bride when the trumpet sounds. An understanding of the Jewish wedding will enlighten us greatly. Most of the Scriptures that deal with Christ coming for his bride coincide perfectly with the Jewish customs of a man taking a bride. As you will see, an understanding of these customs is the key to a better understanding of the truths concerning the rapture and of our becoming the bride of Christ. As with all types in the Bible, it teaches a pre-tribulation rapture.

The following is a step by step process of how a Jewish man got his bride in Bible days according to Jewish customs. I want you to see how it coincides with Bible prophecy and I trust that its truths will forever reinforce your beliefs concerning the things that are shortly to come to pass!

How a Man Got a Bride in Bible Days
A type of Christ and His church

1. The man would make his offer to purchase his bride.

We see this in the story of Rebekah in Genesis 24.

This offer would be with the permission of her father of course, and there may or may not have been some courting between them. He could even be a complete stranger to her, as in the case of Isaac and Rebekah. The woman could only be his bride if she consented willingly, and a price was paid to her by the groom.

You and I were also purchased at a great price: Acts 20:28 *"...the church of God, which he hath purchased with his own blood."* However, He does not force us to be His bride; we must choose to accept Him and His payment.

Some similarities of Rebekah and a person trusting Christ:

a. She trusted a person she had never seen, just as you and I

24

must trust a Saviour we have only heard about through the Scriptures.

b. She received a free gift. Our salvation is a free gift from God. Romans 6:23 *"... but the gift of God is eternal life through Jesus Christ our Lord.*

c. She left her kingdom for his kingdom. One day you and I will leave earth and enter His Kingdom.

d. It was an act of her own free will. "Whosoever will"

2. Next, a marriage contract would be given.

This contract spells out the conditions, inheritance, and obligations of the marriage. (Jacob had a contract for both of his wives.)

This would be similar to the vows that a husband makes at the alter which shows that even some of our traditions are rooted in Jewish custom. Just as the groom gives the bride a contract, Jesus has given us His word, the Bible. A covenant filled with His promises to us, His bride.

John 14:1-3 Let not your heart be troubled: ye believe in God, believe also in me. In my Father's house are many mansions: if it were not so, I would have told you. I go to prepare a place for you and if I go and prepare a place for you, I will come again, and receive you unto myself; that where I am, there ye may be also.

3. When the bride accepted and received the purchase price, she would be formally betrothed or espoused and then belong to the groom.

The actual ceremony may not take place for months, and there is no physical contact until the ceremony. (Story of Joseph and Mary) Betrothed means contracted for future marriage. Espoused means promised in marriage by contract. She will continue to live with her parents until he returns for her. When you and I accept the free gift of eternal life, we are saved and become the purchased property of Christ immediately, but we have no physical contact, just like Jewish custom. We are espoused to Christ, but are not actually the bride until He comes for us at the rapture.

2 Corinthians 11:22 For I am jealous over you with godly jealousy: for I have espoused you to one husband, that I may present you as a chaste virgin to Christ.

4. The Groom would go back to his father's house to prepare for his new bride. (Prepares a bridal chamber)

a. He leaves the purchase price with her, a kind of guarantee. We get the Holy Spirit as a down payment, as a surety that He is coming back for us. *Ephesians 1:14 Which is the earnest of our inheritance until the redemption of the purchased possession, unto the praise of his glory.* Wow, talk about the eternal security of the believer!

b. He may be gone for quite a while. Our Saviour has been gone for nearly 2000 years now!

c. He promises to return for her. The bride is to watch and wait.

John 14:2-3 "...I go to prepare a place for you. And if I go and prepare a place for you, I will come again, and receive you unto myself; that where I am, there ye may be also."

This passage will mean more to you now than ever before! Jesus has gone back to Heaven, to the Father's house. He is preparing a place for His bride. As soon as it is ready, He is coming back for us! That is the rapture, the end of the church age.

5. The bride-to-be would prepare herself for his sudden return.

a. It is in her marriage contract to do so. Our marriage contract is the Bible. We are to be growing in grace and preparing for His return.

b. She was to purify herself, and keep herself for only him.

2 Corinthians 11:2 For I am jealous over you with godly jealousy: for I have espoused you to one husband, that I may present you as a chaste virgin to Christ.

c. She was to be ready and waiting to go with him at any moment! She was to have her bags packed and be ready to go at a moments notice. We too are to be ready at any moment for the coming of Christ. This is more proof that the rapture is before the Tribulation, and that it could happen any moment. *Luke 12:40 Be ye therefore ready also: for the Son of man cometh at an hour when ye think not.*

Revelation 19:7 Let us be glad and rejoice, and give honour to him: for the marriage of the Lamb is come, and his wife hath made herself ready.

If we would only believe that we are the espoused bride of Christ, it would effect the way that we live. The truth is, most of us are unfaithful and most of God's people do not even faithfully read the word of God, His love letter to us.

6. The bride-to-be would participate in a ritual of being immersed.

What a symbol of baptism…a new convert gets baptized after salvation. Not only does this get the believer into the church, but it is also a beautiful picture of what our Groom did to purchase us.

7. Only the father of the groom would know the date of the wedding.

Not the bride, nor even the groom, it is the father who decides when the house is ready. Truth is, if it were up to us men, we would just elope and live in a shack!

Matthew 24:36 But of that day and hour knoweth no man, no, not the angels of heaven, but my Father only.

8. The woman would light an oil lamp for the groom each night.

This is symbolic of her expecting and hoping he would come that night. It also helped the groom find her window at night, as well as let other men know she was espoused. Hey, does the world's crowd know that you belong to the King of Kings? Oil is also symbolic of the Holy Ghost. The light symbolizes Jesus, the light of the world. Now you will better understand the parable of the ten virgins in Matthew 25 next time you read it. Five had oil and five did not. If oil is a symbol of the Holy Spirit, then five of those virgins were lost and missed the rapture. How sad that is, especially when you realize that the ten virgins are a type of the church. Half (5 of 10) in the church are not saved!

9. When the father decided that it was time, he would send his son to get his bride and would prepare for the ceremony.

a. This announcement was made to the son with the sounding of trumpets. 1 Corinthians 15:51-57, 1 Thessalonians 4:16 and Revelation 4:1 all speak of the rapture occurring with a trumpet.

b. Guests are invited to the wedding.

c. A shout was made at the door…this was the signal for the bride to rush out to meet him, as well as for modesty's sake. The groom would meet her at the door and carry her out. (This may be where we got the tradition of carrying the bride over the threshold) Hey, at the rapture we are caught up! It is very possible, in light of this, that the trumpet is heard only in Heaven.

d. This was usually done at night and in secret. Christ is coming for us "*as a thief in the night.*"

e. The lost world will not even know you left to get married.

10. The wedding ceremony would take place.

At the wedding would be the Rabbi, the Best man, two witnesses, and family and friends. The two witnesses may be the Father and the Holy Ghost. The Rabbi would be the word of God, and the friends would be the Old Testament saints.

11. The couple would enter the bridal chamber and have a seven-day honeymoon.
This symbolizes the seven years we are in Heaven during the Tribulation. What a contrast! The type of Judgment Seat takes place here, where the groom brags on the good of his bride. Jesus will reward His bride and brag on her before all of Heaven. The Judgment Seat is not a place where sin is judged, that was taken care of at Calvary. Jesus Christ already took the punishment for ALL of the believer's sins. The Judgment Seat is where our works are judged. *1 Corinthians 3:13 Every man's work shall be made manifest: for the day shall declare it, because it shall be revealed by fire; and the fire shall try every man's work of what sort it is.*
14 If any man's work abide which he hath built thereupon, he shall receive a reward.
15 If any man's work shall be burned, he shall suffer loss: but he himself shall be saved; yet so as by fire.

How sad that some will be left with nothing but ashes, while others earn a crown. This seven-day honeymoon is a type of the seven years of Tribulation. While we are eating cake in Heaven, the terrible Tribulation is taking place down on earth.
12. At the end of the seven-day honeymoon, the couple would go to their new home.
This would be the time of the marriage supper as well. We would call it a reception today, and it would take place after the wedding, but not in Bible times. In Jewish custom, this supper was held after the honeymoon.

Application:
1. Am I espoused to Christ?
2. Am I faithful to Him?
3. Am I daily making myself ready to meet Him?
4. Am I inviting others to the wedding?
5. Do I expect His coming tonight?
6. Is my lamp shining brightly?

I trust that a deeper understanding of these Jewish customs will help open up the prophetic truths of the Scriptures and that you will strive to be faithful to Jesus Christ.

Jesus began His ministry with a wedding (John 2) and He will end His ministry with a wedding when He comes for His Bride.

THE 70TH WEEK
Chapter 3
Daniel 9:22-27

Daniel 9:22 And he informed me, and talked with me, and said, O Daniel, I am now come forth to give thee skill and understanding.
23 At the beginning of thy supplications the commandment came forth, and I am come to shew thee; for thou art greatly beloved: therefore understand the matter, and consider the vision.
24 Seventy weeks are determined upon thy people and upon thy holy city, to finish the transgression, and to make an end of sins, and to make reconciliation for iniquity, and to bring in everlasting righteousness, and to seal up the vision and prophecy, and to anoint the most Holy.
25 Know therefore and understand, that from the going forth of the commandment to restore and to build Jerusalem unto the Messiah the Prince shall be seven weeks, and threescore and two weeks: the street shall be built again, and the wall, even in troublous times.
26 And after threescore and two weeks shall Messiah be cut off, but not for himself: and the people of the prince that shall come shall destroy the city and the sanctuary; and the end thereof shall be with a flood, and unto the end of the war desolations are determined.
27 And he shall confirm the covenant with many for one week: and in the midst of the week he shall cause the sacrifice and the oblation to cease, and for the overspreading of abominations he shall make it desolate, even until the consummation, and that determined shall be poured upon the desolate.

An understanding of Daniel's 70th week in this passage will greatly help you in grasping the timeline of end time events. Daniel Chapter 9 is probably the most important chapter in all the Bible for the student who is studying the book of Revelation. You simply can not grasp the book of

Revelation without a grasp of the book of Daniel. Daniel Chapter 9 holds one of the keys to the puzzle concerning the end times! Throughout this book you will be hearing the term "Daniel's 70ᵗʰ week." I realize how confusing this can be, so I have devoted the following chapter to the subject. Let me give you a few observations from the passage.

1. Theme of the passage is the 70 weeks.

We see this in verse 24.

2. These "weeks" are literally weeks of years as we see from the context.

Each week represents seven years. Seventy weeks would equal four hundred ninety years total. Remember that Jacob worked seven years for each of his wives. The Bible says in *Genesis 29:27 "fulfill her week,"* speaking of a seven year period of time. So we see that the theme of the passage is the seventy weeks of years determined upon Israel.

3. These weeks have to do with Israel, not the Church.

In verse 24 we see that "*Seventy weeks are determined upon thy people and upon thy holy city,*" and of course, the people are the Jews, and the holy city is Jerusalem. We need to get this settled right from the beginning. The Church is not the subject of these seventy weeks; Israel is the subject of the seventy weeks. The seventy weeks are determined upon Israel, not the church. It is important to understand this.

4. The purpose of these 70 weeks is given in verse 24.

1. To finish the transgression
2. To make an end of sins
3. To make reconciliation
4. To bring in everlasting righteousness
5. To seal up the vision
6. To anoint the most Holy

Have you ever asked yourself why there needs to be the seven-year Tribulation? Well, here is your answer to that question. The Tribulation is the final week of the seventy weeks that is appointed upon Israel. It is to put a final end to sin, bring reconciliation, bring to fulfillment God's prophecy, bring in righteousness, anoint the Lord Jesus Christ as King of Kings and Lord of Lord's, and begin the reign of Christ during the 1000-year Millennium. It is also about redeeming the earth. Man's spirit is redeemed at salvation; our bodies will be redeemed at the rapture, the main harvest. The earth will be redeemed during the Tribulation when the Seven-Sealed Book, the title deed to the earth, is opened. All these things are a part of the purpose of the seventy weeks of years and are for Israel. As already shown, the church will not be here for the 70th week. (See chapter one)

5. 69 of the 70 weeks have already been fulfilled.

In verses 24-26 of our passage, we see this is true. Briefly, the first seven weeks (49 years) took place in Ezra and Nehemiah at the building of the temple and the walls around the city. Then the next 62 weeks (434 years) take place after the building of the wall in Nehemiah until Christ is "cut off" at Calvary. This leaves one week (7 years) yet to be fulfilled after all believers are raptured. Do you see it in the passage? I realize it is a little confusing when you read it because the Lord breaks it up into stages. The first 49 years is before the wall in Nehemiah, the next 434 years is after the wall and ends with Messiah riding into Jerusalem on the donkey just four days before Calvary. That leaves 7 years left to finish the 490 years which are called 70 weeks.

6. Daniel's 70th week is yet to come.

God's time clock stopped for Israel when Christ was "cut off" and crucified at Calvary. One of the reasons we are so confused about the dating of the calendar today is because we have started the New Testament at the birth of Christ, instead of at Calvary. We will deal with that more later. For the last 2000 years we have been in the Church Age. When we get to Revelation Chapter 4, all the saved will be removed and God's time clock will begin again with the final week of seven years we call Daniel's 70th week. The Church Age will be over. Look again at Daniel 9:25-26 and you will see that from the time the command came to restore and build Jerusalem, (483 years before Calvary) until it was completed even in times of trouble and danger, was seven weeks (49 years). Then another 62 weeks (434 years) until Messiah is cut off to pay the sin debt of the world. Have you ever wondered why the people were waiting for the Messiah to ride into Jerusalem on what we call Palm Sunday? *John 12:12-15 On the next day much people that were come to the feast, when they heard that Jesus was coming to Jerusalem, Took branches of palm trees, and went forth to meet him, and cried, Hosanna: Blessed is the King of Israel that cometh in the name of the Lord. And Jesus, when he had found a young ass, sat thereon; as it is written, Fear not, daughter of Sion: behold, thy King cometh, sitting on an ass's colt.*

It is because of this timeline, it was prophesied right to the day when Messiah was to arrive, 483 years after the command to build the wall. Check Ussher's dates in Ezra and Nehemiah and add 33 years till Calvary and it comes out to around 483 years. That is why we read that many of the women in Joseph's and Mary's day were hoping to be the chosen one, and many prophesied of His soon appearing. They did not know the month or day He would be born, but they knew right to the day when the Messiah would enter the city. I say they knew, or maybe I should say, they should have known.

7. This 70th week (seven-year Tribulation) yet to come begins at the rapture in Revelation Chapter 4 and is in two 3 1/2 year periods.

See *Daniel 9:27 And he shall confirm the covenant with many for one week: and in the midst of the week he shall*

34

cause the sacrifice and the oblation to cease, and for the overspreading of abominations he shall make it desolate, even until the consummation, and that determined shall be poured upon the desolate.

It says that in the "midst" or "middle" of the week of seven years, the Antichrist shall enter the temple and end the sacrifices; declare he is God, and break the peace treaty with Israel. This temple shall be built before, or right after the rapture on the very spot that the Dome of the Rock now occupies, and it may in fact be built for the Jews by the Antichrist himself. Is there any question as to why the Dome of the Rock was built there? Do you understand why Jerusalem is such a hot spot in the world? The whole series of end-time events will be consummated in that very spot! They have even put a cemetery in front of the Eastern Gate in hopes of keeping the Messiah from coming through! Matthew 24:15-24 gives reference to what Daniel spoke of and calls this second half of the 70th week the "*great tribulation.*"

Mt 24:15 When ye therefore shall see the abomination of desolation, spoken of by Daniel the prophet, stand in the holy place, (whoso readeth, let him understand:) Then let them which be in Judaea flee into the mountains: Let him which is on the housetop not come down to take any thing out of his house: Neither let him which is in the field return back to take his clothes. And woe unto them that are with child, and to them that give suck in those days! But pray ye that your flight be not in the winter, neither on the sabbath day: For then shall be <u>great tribulation</u>, such as was not since the beginning of the world to this time, no, nor ever shall be. And except those days should be shortened, there should no flesh be saved: but for the elect's sake those days shall be shortened. Then if any man shall say unto you, Lo, here is Christ, or there; believe it not. For there shall arise false

35

Christs, and false prophets, and shall shew great signs and wonders; insomuch that, if it were possible, they shall deceive the very elect.

Israel will be at peace for the first half of the Tribulation. But that peace will end when the Antichrist enters the temple in the "*midst of the week*"; declares he is God, and expects to receive worship from Israel as their Messiah. All is well until the two witnesses, Moses and Elijah, left for dead in the street 3 ½ days earlier, come back to life and ascend back to Heaven in front of the 144,000 Jewish men who are assembled there for Passover. It is at that moment that they get saved and give glory to God! *Revelation 11:11-13 And after three days and an half the Spirit of life from God entered into them, and they stood upon their feet; and great fear fell upon them which saw them. And they heard a great voice from heaven saying unto them, Come up hither. And they ascended up to heaven in a cloud; and their enemies beheld them. And the same hour was there a great earthquake, and the tenth part of the city fell, and in the earthquake were slain of men seven thousand: and the remnant were affrighted, and <u>gave glory to the God of heaven</u>.*

II Thessalonians 2:4 also speaks of the defiling of the temple at the middle of the Tribulation. *Who opposeth and exalteth himself above all that is called God, or that is worshipped; so that he as God sitteth in the temple of God, shewing himself that he is God.* This happens right at the middle of the Tribulation, in the "*midst of the week*."

The following passage is also applicable to this period of time we call the middle of the Tribulation. Scripture calls it the "*midst of the week*."

Revelation 13:5-6 And there was given unto him a mouth speaking great things and blasphemies; and power was given unto him to continue forty and two months. And he opened his mouth in blasphemy against God, to blaspheme his name, and his tabernacle, and them that dwell in heaven.

Remember, there is a false trinity at work here. Just as God is a Trinity: the Father, Son, and Holy Ghost; Satan has his false trinity: Satan, antichrist and the false prophet. In Revelation 12:6-9 we learn that Satan loses access to Heaven right at the middle of the Tribulation. I believe it is at this time that Satan moves Antichrist to go to Israel and defile the temple (abomination of desolation) and eventually break the peace treaty and declare war on Israel. It is here that the mark of the beast in instituted as well as a record of the first people that get saved, the 144,000 Jews.

I realize this is some deep stuff I have just mentioned, and I may not have backed it all up with Scripture, but we shall deal with some of these things later on.

Let me summarize what we learned in this chapter:

1. The 70th week of Daniel Chapter 9 is the seven-year period we call the Tribulation.

2. The Tribulation (70th week) is for Israel.

3. The Tribulation (70th week) has nothing to do with the church.

4. The Tribulation (70th week) is in two equal parts.

1st half is peace for Israel while the whole world is under a dictatorship and one-world order.

2nd half is the "Time of Jacob's trouble" (Jer 30:7) the Great Tribulation for Israel.

5. Daniel's 70th week begins right after the rapture with the signing of the peace treaty with Israel. (Daniel 9:27)

6. Keep your eyes on Israel!

**Prophecy is
History told in
advance
It is
The Future pre-
written**

THREE INTERPRETATIONS OF SCRIPTURE
Chapter 4

There are three ways to interpret Scripture. If you will grasp this, it will forever change the way you study the Bible. The truth is, many of you are already looking at passages in the Bible in the way I am going to describe, but you do not realize you are doing so. If I can get you to understand the three ways to look at Scripture, you will be shocked how the Bible will open up to you like never before. What I am talking about is nothing new, and it is not some strange doctrine. It is the way Jesus looked at Scripture, as well as Peter, Paul and about every preacher you have ever listened to. However, most folks have never sat down and analyzed what I am talking about. I propose that if you understand that Scripture is to be looked at three ways, and you know that as you begin to read, you can be looking for these interpretations in advance. I believe the more aware of this we are, the more the Lord will show us as we read.

I believe there are three ways to look at a verse or passage in the Bible. I believe all three views could be different and yet all three views be 100% true. You are thinking, how is this possible? Well, let me give you the three ways to interpret Scripture and I think you will see what I mean.

1. The literal interpretation.
2. The figurative interpretation.
3. The prophetic interpretation.

I can almost hear some sighs of relief out there as you realize I am not teaching some strange new doctrine after all. Yet, so few folks have ever really had these three views of interpreting the Scripture explained or taught to them. Most simply stumble around in their Bible reading and hope for the best. Well, it is time to get an understanding of how to study and read this supernatural book we call the Bible.

Nothing has helped my study quite as much as an understanding of these three ways to look at the Scripture. Often you hear of men who argue and fight over the interpretation of a passage of Scripture. Funny thing is, sometimes both men are right but both are wrong at the same time! In other words, one guy states the literal interpretation while the other is looking at it figuratively. Both may be exactly right in what they are saying. However, each are wrong to reject the other's interpretation. For example, one guy says the days in Genesis Chapter 1 are literal 24 hour days. For the record, I agree 100% with that belief. I too believe they were literal 24 hour days. However, another guy comes and teaches that those days are prophetic of 1000 year periods of history. I want to go on record today that I believe that to be 100% true as well! In fact there will be a chapter later in the book on that very topic. Now, can both views be correct? Of course they can. The first view is the literal interpretation. The second view is the prophetic interpretation. Both views are different, but both are the truth.

There are three ways to look at Scriptures.
1. Literally
2. Figurative/typically
3. Prophetically

Now, the 3rd view is often the hardest to see. I have been studying prophecy for many years, so things seem to jump out at me more easily than for others. I am not saying that in every verse or passage you read you will find a figurative or a prophetic truth. I am saying that we ought to be always LOOKING for it. Jesus interpreted Scriptures in this manner.

John 3:14 And as Moses lifted up the serpent in the wilderness, even so must the Son of man be lifted up:
John 6:49 Your fathers did eat manna in the wilderness, and are dead.
Matthew 12:40 For as Jonas was three days and three nights in the whale's belly; so shall the Son of man be three days and three nights in the heart of the earth.

In all of these places the Lord took a literal Bible story and used it figuratively to teach a truth. The Apostle Peter used the creative week in Genesis 1 and interpreted it prophetically.

2 Peter 3:3-8 Knowing this first, that there shall come in the last days scoffers, walking after their own lusts, And saying, Where is the promise of his coming? for since the fathers fell asleep, all things continue as they were <u>from the beginning of the creation</u>. For this they willingly are ignorant of, that by the word of God the heavens were of old, and the earth <u>standing out of the water and in the water:</u> Whereby the world that then was, being <u>overflowed with water</u>, perished: But the heavens and the earth, which are now, by the same word are kept in store, reserved unto fire against the day of judgment and perdition of ungodly men. But, beloved, be not ignorant of this one thing, that <u>one day is with the Lord as a thousand years, and a thousand years as one day</u>.

The Apostle Paul used the Old Testament figuratively:
For it is written, that Abraham had two sons, the one by a bondmaid, the other by a freewoman. But he who was of the bondwoman was born after the flesh; but he of the freewoman was by promise. Which things are an allegory: for these are the two covenants; the one from the mount Sinai, which gendereth to bondage, which is Agar. For this Agar is mount Sinai in Arabia, and answereth to Jerusalem

which now is, and is in bondage with her children. But Jerusalem which is above is free, which is the mother of us all. For it is written, Rejoice, thou barren that bearest not; break forth and cry, thou that travailest not: for the desolate hath many more children than she which hath an husband. Now we, brethren, as Isaac was, are the children of promise. (Galatians 4:22-28)

Do you see it? Paul is very obviously looking at Scriptures in the Old Testament in a figurative and sometimes prophetic way. So it is very right and wise that you and I should do the same. I could go on and give example after example, but I think I have made my point.

I would venture to guess that 95% of the folks reading this book have heard a sermon about being a lukewarm Christian at least once and probably more than once in their life. The message comes from this verse:

Revelation 3:15 I know thy works, that thou art neither cold nor hot: I would thou wert cold or hot.

I have preached this more than once myself. Regardless of where you heard it, the message was no doubt the same. We should strive in our walk with God to not become a "lukewarm" Christian. The interesting thing about it is that the passage used in Revelation 3 is not speaking about an individual believer at all. The passage is speaking about a church becoming lukewarm, the church of the Laodiceans to be exact. That is the literal interpretation. However, it is perfectly right to use the passage figuratively and prophetically when appropriate. After all, the whole Bible is filled with figurative lessons for us.

There are many figures and types in the Bible that have a prophetic interpretation. We will look at several of them in a later chapter, but for the sake of helping us understand the three interpretations, let's look at a couple here. Since we were just looking at the lukewarm church in Revelation, let's

42

go ahead and use the seven churches listed in Revelation 2 and 3 for our first example.

The Seven Churches
Revelation 2 and 3

1. Literal interpretation

These were seven literal churches that existed in that day. They give us insight into Christ's ownership and relationship to the church. They also show us the relationship between the pastor of the church and the Lord. These churches show us what a church ought to be, as well as some things a church ought not to be. This is a simple literal interpretation. These seven churches all existed in 96 A.D. when John got the Revelation from the Lord while on the island of Patmos.

2. Figurative interpretation

Truths concerning these seven churches can also be applied to the Christian life. For instance, the church in Ephesus had left its first love. You and I ought to examine our own lives. Do we have the love for Christ and a love for souls that we once had? Take some time to consider the good and bad about each church and see how you measure up. See, this is looking at the seven churches figuratively.

3. Prophetic interpretation

Though I believe that these are literal churches that existed in John's day, **I believe the main prophetic teaching concerning these churches is that they are the seven ages of church history.** Let me give you some reasons I am certain of this:

A) Because the first verse of the Revelation shows that it is a prophetic book of things to come.

See *Revelation 1:1 The Revelation of Jesus Christ, which God gave unto him, to shew unto his servants things which must shortly come to pass; and he sent and signified it by his angel unto his servant John:*

B) Because of its chronological order in the book. The

43

rapture takes place in Chapter 4 right after the last of the seven churches is mentioned. And that last church is a cold and dead church that the Bible says will exist at the rapture.

C) Looking back, we can clearly see all seven of these church ages in history.

So there we have an example of the seven churches in Revelation 2 and 3 interpreted three different ways and yet all perfectly legitimate and right. The Bible is filled with types and figures to help us understand truth. Did you ever consider the prophetic lessons concerning Mary, Martha, and Lazarus? As you know, Mary and Martha were sisters and Lazarus was their brother. There are several passages in the Bible where they are mentioned interacting with the Lord. There are some obvious and interesting types and prophetic lessons we can learn from them. For instance, the passage where Martha is busy in the kitchen and Mary is sitting at the feet of Jesus.

Luke 10:38-42 Now it came to pass, as they went, that he entered into a certain village: and a certain woman named Martha received him into her house. And she had a sister called Mary, which also sat at Jesus' feet, and heard his word. But Martha was cumbered about much serving, and came to him, and said, Lord, dost thou not care that my sister hath left me to serve alone? bid her therefore that she help me. And Jesus answered and said unto her, Martha, Martha, thou art careful and troubled about many things: But one thing is needful: and Mary hath chosen that good part, which shall not be taken away from her.

This was certainly a literal event that happened during the life of Christ, but there is a figurative lesson taught here too. The lesson is about servitude and worship. We certainly need to be about both worshiping and serving, but it is plain which is most important. Then we have this passage about Mary, Martha, and Lazarus:

Now a certain man was sick, named <u>Lazarus</u>, of Bethany, the town of <u>Mary</u> and her sister Martha. (It was that Mary which anointed the Lord with ointment, and wiped his feet with her hair, whose brother Lazarus was sick.) Therefore his sisters sent unto him, saying, Lord, behold, he whom thou lovest is sick. When Jesus heard that, he said, This sickness is not unto death, but for the glory of God, that the Son of God might be glorified thereby. Now Jesus loved <u>Martha</u>, and her sister, and Lazarus. When he had heard therefore that he was sick, he abode two days still in the same place where he was. Then after that saith he to his disciples, Let us go into Judaea again. His disciples say unto him, Master, the Jews of late sought to stone thee; and goest thou thither again? (John 11:1-8)

This is also a literal event that happened during the life of Christ. The story goes on all the way through verse 45 if you want to read it all. It is even mentioned in several other Scriptures. There are not only figurative lessons here, but a tremendous prophetic interpretation as well. Consider this from the passage:

<u>Martha</u> is a type of the Gentile/church-age saints. When Jesus showed up, she went out first and met the Lord. There is the rapture. Martha, representing the church-age saints goes out first. <u>Lazarus</u> would represent "the dead in Christ rise first." Wow, interesting is it not?

<u>Mary</u>: She represents the Jews. She comes along later, after Martha is gone. You see, when the rapture takes place and the church-age saints are removed from the earth, God is once again going to turn His attention to the Jews! God is not done with them!

Notice in this passage:

John 11:33-35 When Jesus therefore saw her weeping, and the Jews also weeping which came with her, <u>he groaned in</u>

45

the spirit, and was troubled, And said, Where have ye laid him? They said unto him, Lord, come and see. Jesus wept.

We see in these verses that Christ has a deep love for the Jews.

In closing this chapter, let me give you some Scriptures that prove that the Bible is a book filled with many figures and types and shadows of future events.

Col 2:16-17 Let no man therefore judge you in meat, or in drink, or in respect of an holyday, or of the new moon, or of the sabbath days: Which are a shadow of things to come; but the body is of Christ.

1 Corinthians 10:1-4 Moreover, brethren, I would not that ye should be ignorant, how that all our fathers were under the cloud, and all passed through the sea; And were all baptized unto Moses in the cloud and in the sea; And did all eat the same spiritual meat; And did all drink the same spiritual drink: for they drank of that spiritual Rock that followed them: and that Rock was Christ.

The wanderings of the children of Israel are all types and figures for us today.

Heb 8:5 Who serve unto the example and shadow of heavenly things, as Moses was admonished of God when he was about to make the tabernacle: for, See, saith he, that thou make all things according to the pattern shewed to thee in the mount.

Heb 9:24 For Christ is not entered into the holy places made with hands, which are the figures of the true; but into heaven itself, now to appear in the presence of God for us:

Heb 10:1 For the law having a shadow of good things to come, and not the very image of the things, can never with those sacrifices which they offered year by year continually make the comers thereunto perfect.

Heb 11:19 Accounting that God was able to raise him up, even from the dead; from whence also he received him in a figure.

A SUMMARY OF THE SEVEN FEASTS OF THE LORD

Chapter 5

In Chapter 1, we learned ten absolute proofs of a pre-tribulation rapture of the saints. In Chapter 2, we looked at a vivid illustration of the rapture by way of the Jewish wedding. We learned that the customs of Israel revolve around Biblical truths. There can be no doubt about the fact that Scripture teaches a pre-tribulation rapture. In Chapter 3, we looked at Daniel Chapter 9 and got an understanding of the 70th week as well as some very deep theological truths that we shall look at in more detail later. In Chapter 4, we saw that the Bible can be interpreted three ways: literally, figuratively, and prophetically. If you have skipped any of these preceding chapters, I strongly urge you to go back and read them. There are some principles there that will help you, even if you are a seasoned prophecy student.

Now that we have gotten a handle on some basics of the return of the Lord, we are going to move on to some very exciting prophetic truths in the word of God. In this chapter we are going to look at the Seven Feasts of the Lord. **I believe <u>the seven feasts are the Bible's prophetic calendar.</u>** I believe an understanding of these seven feasts is the key that unlocks the door to prophecy. You will see what I mean in the next few chapters, but for now let's get a basic summary of these seven feasts. Remember, there are three ways to look at Scripture. There are some wonderful figurative and prophetic truths waiting to be uncovered here, but we always want to be sure we see the literal view first.

The seven feasts are mentioned in several places in

Scripture. For instance, Passover is mentioned in Exodus 12 as well as in I Corinthians 5:7 and a number of other places. However, we have a list of all seven of the feasts in Leviticus 23. These seven feasts were given to Moses right before and during the exodus from Egypt.

FIRST FEAST
Feast of Passover
Leviticus 23:1-5

And the LORD spake unto Moses, saying, Speak unto the children of Israel, and say unto them, Concerning the feasts of the LORD, which ye shall proclaim to be holy convocations, even these are my feasts. Six days shall work be done: but the seventh day is the sabbath of rest, an holy convocation; ye shall do no work therein: it is the sabbath of the LORD in all your dwellings. These are the feasts of the LORD, even holy convocations, which ye shall proclaim in their seasons. In the fourteenth day of the first month at even is <u>the LORD'S passover</u>. (Leviticus 23:1-5)

Moses was given the instructions about the Passover way back in Exodus 12. If you recall, the last of the ten plagues that God brought upon Egypt to free the children of Israel was the death of the firstborn of every family. Moses was instructed to tell the people to take a male lamb of the first year, a lamb without spot or blemish. This was to be done on the 10th of their month Nisan. The lamb had to be watched for four days to be sure it was not sick. Then, on the 14th day of the month was Passover. They were to kill the lamb and put the blood on the door posts of the house. The blood would save the firstborn of the household. The figurative meaning is almost impossible to miss. The lamb represents

Christ and His shed blood that saves us from death and hell. Imagine being alive in that day and experiencing the horror of that night! But that is nothing like the horror of missing salvation through Christ and awakening in hellfire!

It is also worth noting here that the month of Nisan was changed from the seventh month on their calendar year to the first month. See Exodus 12:2. In other words, before Exodus 12, the seventh month of their calendar was Nisan. After Exodus 12, Nisan was the first month. Passover is always on the 14th of Nisan and is always a full moon. The Jewish calendar is based on the moon and does not synchronize with our calendar. (This will be dealt with later.) The 1st of the month is the new moon; the 14th of the month is a full moon. The Israelites put the blood on the door post on a full moon. Jesus went to the cross of Calvary on a full moon.

SECOND FEAST
Feast of Unleavened Bread
Leviticus 23:6-8

And on the fifteenth day of the same month is the feast of unleavened bread unto the LORD: seven days ye must eat unleavened bread. In the first day ye shall have an holy convocation: ye shall do no servile work therein. But ye shall offer an offering made by fire unto the LORD seven days: in the seventh day is an holy convocation: ye shall do no servile work therein. (Leviticus 23:6-8)

This second feast was also given to Moses before the Israelites left Egypt. We see it here:
(Exodus 12:15-18) Seven days shall ye eat unleavened bread; even the first day ye shall put away leaven out of your

49

houses: for whosoever eateth leavened bread from the first day until the seventh day, that soul shall be cut off from Israel. And in the first day there shall be an holy convocation, and in the seventh day there shall be an holy convocation to you; no manner of work shall be done in them, save that which every man must eat, that only may be done of you. And ye shall observe the feast of unleavened bread; for in this selfsame day have I brought your armies out of the land of Egypt: therefore shall ye observe this day in your generations by an ordinance for ever. In the first month, on the fourteenth day of the month at even, ye shall eat unleavened bread, until the one and twentieth day of the month at even.

The second feast is the Feast of Unleavened Bread. It started at the end of Passover (15th) and went until the 21st. For seven days the Jews could not eat anything that contained leaven. In fact, they actually had to remove all leaven from their homes. They could not even have it in their cabinets. They had to sweep their houses clean of every crumb. There were a couple reasons for this.

1. Leaven is a type of sin. After being delivered by the blood, we are to get sin (leaven) out of our lives.

2. They had to leave Egypt in great haste! There was no time to wait for the bread to rise, thus the unleavened bread. They ate the Passover meal in haste, with their staffs in their hands ready to flee at any moment.

Exodus 12:11 And thus shall ye eat it; with your loins girded, your shoes on your feet, and your staff in your hand; and ye shall eat it in haste: it is the LORD'S passover.

THIRD FEAST
Feast of Firstfruits
Leviticus 23:9-14

And the LORD spake unto Moses, saying, Speak unto the children of Israel, and say unto them, When ye be come into the land which I give unto you, and shall reap the harvest thereof, then ye shall bring a sheaf of the firstfruits of your harvest unto the priest: And he shall wave the sheaf before the LORD, to be accepted for you: on the morrow after the sabbath the priest shall wave it. And ye shall offer that day when ye wave the sheaf an he lamb without blemish of the first year for a burnt offering unto the LORD. And the meat offering thereof shall be two tenth deals of fine flour mingled with oil, an offering made by fire unto the LORD for a sweet savour: and the drink offering thereof shall be of wine, the fourth part of an hin. And ye shall eat neither bread, nor parched corn, nor green ears, until the selfsame day that ye have brought an offering unto your God: it shall be a statute for ever throughout your generations in all your dwellings. (Leviticus 23:9-14)

Feast of Firstfruits is always the first day of the week (Sunday) after Passover. Literally, it was a time of offering the first fruits of the harvest unto God in thanksgiving. This is during the barley harvest. It takes place during the Feast of Unleavened Bread which lasts for seven days. The children of Israel crossed the Red Sea on this very day. In the New Testament, Christ rose from the grave on this same day! Christ died on Passover on the 14th of Nisan and rose three days later on the Feast of Firstfruits, the 17th of Nisan.

FOURTH FEAST
Feast of Pentecost
Leviticus 23:15-16

And ye shall count unto you from the morrow after the

51

sabbath, from the day that ye brought the sheaf of the wave offering; seven sabbaths shall be complete: Even unto the morrow after the seventh sabbath shall ye number fifty days; and ye shall offer a new meat offering unto the LORD.

Fifty days from the Feast of Firstfruits is the Feast of Pentecost. This is the fourth feast of the Lord. In Israel the wheat harvest is centered around this time. The church would be empowered on this very day in Acts 2. Pentecost or Shavuot is also called the Feast of Weeks and Feast of Harvest. It was celebrated on the fiftieth day after Firstfruits. Pentecost is traditionally a time of giving thanks and presenting offerings for the summer wheat harvest in Israel. The name "Feast of Weeks" was given because God commanded the Jews in Leviticus 23:15-16, to count seven full weeks (or 49 days) beginning on the second day of Passover, and then present offerings of new grain to the Lord as a lasting ordinance. Jews believe that it was on Pentecost when Moses brought the Ten Commandments from the Mount.

FIFTH FEAST
Feast of Trumpets
Leviticus 23:23-25

And the LORD spake unto Moses, saying, Speak unto the children of Israel, saying, In the seventh month, in the first day of the month, shall ye have a sabbath, a memorial of blowing of trumpets, an holy convocation. Ye shall do no servile work therein: but ye shall offer an offering made by fire unto the LORD. (Leviticus 23:23-25)

Feast of Trumpets is the fifth feast. It begins at the new moon on day one of the month Tishri. The Jewish calendar is based on the moon. Our calendar is based upon the sun. The Jewish month begins on the new moon. Feast of

Trumpets would begin at the sighting of the new moon in the sky and would be announced with the blowing of trumpets. The 1st of Tishri is in late September or early October on our calendar. This is the fall of the year. The first three feasts were all in the spring, with the first three in the first month, the month of Nisan, which is late March or early April for us. The last three feasts are all in the fall and all in the month of Tishri. These revolve around the fruit harvest. The first four feasts have already been fulfilled by Christ. The last three fall feasts have not yet been fulfilled. I believe the Feast of Trumpets is prophetic of the rapture. We will look at this prophetically in depth later, but let me share a few things as to why I believe this feast represents the rapture.

1. It is the next feast of the seven awaiting fulfillment, just as the rapture is the next event on God's time table.

2. It is the one feast that no man knows the day or hour that it begins. Let me explain. Feast of trumpets is the only feast that begins on the new moon which is the first day of the month. This feast did not begin until the representatives of the temple, usually two men who were sent to the hillside, had actually seen the sliver of the new moon in the sky and reported back to the High Priest. It was then that the trumpet would be blown and the feast would officially begin.

3. It is the feast that fits the description of the rapture with the blowing of trumpets.

For this we say unto you by the word of the Lord, that we which are alive and remain unto the coming of the Lord shall not prevent them which are asleep. For the Lord himself shall descend from heaven with a shout, with the voice of the archangel, and with the trump of God: and the dead in Christ shall rise first: Then we which are alive and remain shall be caught up together with them in the clouds, to meet the Lord in the air: and so shall we ever be with the Lord. Wherefore comfort one another with these words.

(1 Thessalonians 4:15-18)

After this I looked, and, behold, a door was opened in heaven: and the first voice which I heard was as it were of a trumpet talking with me; which said, Come up hither, and I will shew thee things which must be hereafter.
(Revelation 4:1)
In a moment, in the twinkling of an eye, at the last trump: for the trumpet shall sound, and the dead shall be raised incorruptible, and we shall be changed. (1Corinthians 15:52)
4. It is the beginning of fruit harvest. The rapture is a harvest of souls.

SIXTH FEAST
Day of Atonement
Leviticus 23:26-32

And the LORD spake unto Moses, saying, Also on the tenth day of this seventh month there shall be a day of atonement: it shall be an holy convocation unto you; and ye shall afflict your souls, and offer an offering made by fire unto the LORD. And ye shall do no work in that same day: for it is a day of atonement, to make an atonement for you before the LORD your God. For whatsoever soul it be that shall not be afflicted in that same day, he shall be cut off from among his people. And whatsoever soul it be that doeth any work in that same day, the same soul will I destroy from among his people. Ye shall do no manner of work: it shall be a statute for ever throughout your generations in all your dwellings. It shall be unto you a sabbath of rest, and ye shall afflict your souls: in the ninth day of the month at even, from even unto even, shall ye celebrate your sabbath. (Leviticus 23:26-32)

The Jews call this sixth Feast, Yom Kippur. It is their most holy day of the year. It is that one day of the year when the High Priest goes into the Holy of Holies and offers a sacrifice for the nation of Israel. Feast of Trumpets occurs on the 1st day of the month Tishri. Day of Atonement occurs on the 10th of the same month. Five days later, on the 15th, the Feast of Tabernacles begins. It is my personal opinion that Christ comes back to the earth at the second coming on the Day of Atonement.

SEVENTH FEAST
Feast of Tabernacles
Leviticus 23:33-37

And the LORD spake unto Moses, saying, Speak unto the children of Israel, saying, The fifteenth day of this seventh month shall be the feast of tabernacles for seven days unto the LORD. On the first day shall be an holy convocation: ye shall do no servile work therein. Seven days ye shall offer an offering made by fire unto the LORD: on the eighth day shall be an holy convocation unto you; and ye shall offer an offering made by fire unto the LORD: it is a solemn assembly; and ye shall do no servile work therein. These are the feasts of the LORD, which ye shall proclaim to be holy convocations, to offer an offering made by fire unto the LORD, a burnt offering, and a meat offering, a sacrifice, and drink offerings, every thing upon his day:
(Leviticus 23:33-37)

This seventh and final feast takes place on the 15th of Tishri. Just five days after the Day of Atonement. The Jews would all assemble together, put up their tents, and dwell in them for seven days. Sometimes it is called Feast of Booths. Tabernacle literally means "to dwell with." God wants to tabernacle or "dwell" with us. I believe this feast is a type of the 1000 year Millennium, the 7th day of the creative week in Genesis 1.

This chart lists the seven feasts

1. Feast of Passover	Nisan 10th - 14th (our March or April)
2. Feast of Unleavened Bread	Nisan 15th - 21st , 7 days
3. Feast of Firstfruits	First day of week after Passover
4. Feast of Pentecost	Fifty days after Firstfruits
Four Month Gap Here	
5. Feasts of Trumpets	1st day of Seventh Month
6. Feast of Day of Atonement	10th day of Seventh Month
7. Feast of Tabernacles	15th day of Seventh Month

A Few Observations

1. The seven feasts all take place in seven months beginning in Nisan and ending in Tishri. The number seven is God's number of completion.

2. The first four feast are spring feasts and were all fulfilled by Christ.

3. The last three feasts are fall feasts and all in the month of Tishri and are yet to be fulfilled.

THE JOURNEYS OF THE CHRISTIAN LIFE
The Seven Feasts Looked at Figuratively
Chapter 6

For many years one of my favorite topics to preach about has been a series called "The Journeys of the Christian Life." However, it was not until I began preaching prophecy that I saw the prophetic connection between this series and the coming of the Lord.

In this chapter I want to give you a summary of that series before we move on to a more in depth prophetic interpretation. I think this figurative interpretation of the seven feasts will be quite enlightening to you. You see, these journeys of the children of Israel, and the feasts of the Lord are mentioned all through the Bible. The problem is that most of us have missed the significance of it. I said earlier that the seven feasts are the key to understanding prophecy. Let me say this too: **The seven feasts are the key to understanding the entire Christian life!** In this chapter we are going to see a clear picture of not only salvation, but a clear picture of the church and how one gets into it. We will see the importance of the word of God as well as the principle of God's divine order of things. So let's begin the journey where it starts, with Moses on the mountain of God.

Now Moses kept the flock of Jethro his father in law, the priest of Midian: and he led the flock to the backside of the desert, and came to the mountain of God, even to Horeb. And the angel of the LORD appeared unto him in a flame of fire out of the midst of a bush: and he looked, and, behold, the bush burned with fire, and the bush was not consumed. And

Moses said, I will now turn aside, and see this great sight, why the bush is not burnt. And when the LORD saw that he turned aside to see, God called unto him out of the midst of the bush, and said, Moses, Moses. And he said, Here am I. And he said, Draw not nigh hither: put off thy shoes from off thy feet, for the place whereon thou standest is holy ground. Moreover he said, I am the God of thy father, the God of Abraham, the God of Isaac, and the God of Jacob. And Moses hid his face; for he was afraid to look upon God. And the LORD said, I have surely seen the affliction of my people which are in Egypt, and have heard their cry by reason of their taskmasters; for I know their sorrows; And I am come down to deliver them out of the hand of the Egyptians, and to bring them up out of that land unto a good land and a large, unto a land flowing with milk and honey; unto the place of the Canaanites, and the Hittites, and the Amorites, and the Perizzites, and the Hivites, and the Jebusites. Now therefore, behold, the cry of the children of Israel is come unto me: and I have also seen the oppression wherewith the Egyptians oppress them. Come now therefore, and I will send thee unto Pharaoh, that thou mayest bring forth my people the children of Israel out of Egypt. (Exodus 3:1-10)

The theme throughout the entire Bible is that God wants to fellowship with man. Get hold of that truth and it will change your life! The very reason God created man was for the purpose of fellowship. Remember what the very last feast is? The Feast of Tabernacles right? Remember what the definition of Tabernacles is? It means to dwell with, "to tabernacle" means "to dwell with." The end of the seven feasts is when God gets man to dwell with Him, and to fellowship and spend time with Him. That is the whole Christian life in a nutshell. That is the whole creation in a nutshell.

Look at these Scriptures:

Revelation 4:11 Thou art worthy, O Lord, to receive glory and honour and power: for thou hast <u>created all things, and for thy pleasure they are and were created.</u>

Psalm 102:18 This shall be written for the generation to come: and the people which shall be <u>created shall praise the LORD.</u>

1 Corinthians 1:9 God is faithful, by whom ye were called unto the <u>fellowship of his Son Jesus Christ our Lord.</u>

Php 3:10 That I may know him, and the power of his resurrection, and <u>the fellowship of his sufferings,</u> being made conformable unto his death;

1 John 1:3-6 That which we have seen and heard declare we unto you, that ye also may have fellowship with us: <u>and truly our fellowship is with the Father, and with his Son Jesus Christ.</u> And these things write we unto you, that your joy may be full. This then is the message which we have heard of him, and declare unto you, that God is light, and in him is no darkness at all. If we say that we have <u>fellowship with him,</u> and walk in darkness, we lie, and do not the truth:

What a tremendous privilege man was afforded. He was given the honor of fellowshipping with the God of the universe! The Scriptures I quoted above tell us that man was made for this very purpose. One of the reasons folks are so depressed today is they do not know why they were created.

In the book of Genesis, God created Adam and Eve. The Bible says that God and Adam fellowshipped together. One day God showed up and called to Adam, but he had hid himself from the presence of the Lord because of sin. God killed a lamb, shed its blood, and made skins for Adam and Eve as a figure/type of the Lamb of God that would one day come into the world and pay the sin debt of all men on the cross. (See Rev 13:8) My friend, that is the theme of the Bible from Genesis to Revelation. God made man to fellowship with Him. When man sinned, that fellowship was broken. God sent His own Son into the world and He *"became sin for us"* that we could place our faith in Him and be saved from the penalty of sin which is hell. When you place your faith in Jesus Christ, that fellowship is restored. Man can once again communicate with his creator. We can "tabernacle" with God. But how sad it is that the average born again Christian today spends very little time in fellowship with God. It seems a shame that after all God did to get man back, He gets short-changed. Man takes that gift of salvation and walks right back into Egypt (the world) and lives like nothing happened. I think the saddest verse in all the Bible is this: *Jeremiah 2:32 Can a maid forget her ornaments, or a bride her attire? yet my people have forgotten me days without number.*

Dear friend, if you are not sure that you are a child of God, go immediately to the last chapter in this book and read about how to be sure you have eternal life. If you are a child of God, I pray that this chapter will enlighten you and bring conviction upon you as to your great purpose here in this life. That purpose is to bring glory to and fellowship with the creator and the God of the universe.

The seven feasts and the journeys of the children of Israel are going to illustrate the Christian life and what it is all about. We start in Exodus 3 with Moses on the mountain of God. *"And God sought for a man"* and that man was Moses. That is how God works; He uses men. Moses had spent forty years in Egypt which is a type of the world. Moses then spent forty years on the back side of the desert as a shepherd. God then called Moses to go back to Egypt to deliver the Israelites from bondage. Moses is a type of a preacher whom God uses to deliver souls from hell and bring them into the kingdom and fellowship of God. Remember, Tabernacles is the end of the journey of the Christian life, just as it is the last of the seven feasts. It pictures dwelling in the presence of God. Now, let me give you some types in the story that explain the whole journey of the Christian life.

1. Egypt is a type of the world.

Everyone begins here. All men are born into this world as lost sinners in need of a Saviour.

Romans 3:10 As it is written, There is <u>none righteous</u>, no, not one:

Romans 3:23 For <u>all have sinned</u>, and come short of the glory of God;

Romans 5:12 Wherefore, as by one man sin entered into the world, and death by sin; and so <u>death passed upon all men</u>, for that all have sinned:

2. Getting the blood applied to the "doorpost" is a type of salvation.

This is what saves you from sin. This is the Feast of Passover.

1 Corinthians 5:7 Purge out therefore the old leaven, that ye may be a new lump, as ye are unleavened. For even <u>Christ our passover</u> is sacrificed for us.

Exodus 12:13 And the blood shall be to you for a token upon the houses where ye are: <u>and when I see the blood, I will pass over you</u>, and the plague shall not be upon you to destroy you, when I smite the land of Egypt.

1 Peter 1:19 But with the precious blood of Christ, as of a lamb without blemish and without spot

John 3:16 For God so loved the world, that he gave his only begotten Son, that whosoever believeth in him should not perish, but have everlasting life.

The first step of the journey is to get the blood on the doorpost; this is the beginning. Once you have done that, you are still in Egypt but are now ready for the next stage of the journey. You cannot skip this step and expect to arrive at the promised land one day! Pharaoh and his army tried and were drowned in the baptismal waters of the Red Sea.

3. The new believer begins getting sin out of his life symbolized by the seven days of the Feast of Unleavened Bread.

The feast lasted seven days, because it is the number of perfection and that is what growth in grace is all about... becoming holy and useful to God. Secondly, it lasted seven days because it is a process that will not be complete until you get to the end of your journey and stand in His presence. This second step of the Christian life is symbolized by the second feast.

4. Crossing the Red Sea of baptism puts us into the church.

Acts 7:38 This is he, that was in the <u>church in the wilderness</u> with the angel which spake to him in the mount Sina, and with our fathers: who received the lively oracles to give unto us:

1 Corinthians 10:1-4 Moreover, brethren, I would not that ye should be ignorant, how that all our fathers were under the cloud, and all passed through the sea; And were all <u>baptized unto Moses</u> in the cloud and in the sea; And did all eat the same spiritual meat; And did all drink the same spiritual drink: for they drank of that spiritual Rock that followed them: and that Rock was Christ.

This is the next step of the journey yet so many today do not think the church is important. Many skip this step and try to go straight to the land of Canaan. Canaan is the promised land and is figurative of the victorious life where the believer is yielded to God and lives by faith. God ordained the church and commissioned it. It is not God's will for you to ignore the assembly. The children of Israel were called a congregation which is an assembly. By the way, they were NOT called a church until they crossed the Red Sea. Notice the reason why God did not allow them to go directly to Caanan:

Exodus 13:17-18 And it came to pass, when Pharaoh had let the people go, that God led them not through the way of the land of the Philistines, although that was near; for God said, Lest peradventure the people repent when they see war, and they return to Egypt: But God led the people about, through the way of the wilderness of the Red sea: and the children of Israel went up harnessed out of the land of Egypt.

Friend, you and I were not ready to go to battle when we first left Egypt either.

5. The crossing of the Red Sea was on the Feast of Firstfruits.

They crossed the Red Sea three days after Passover on what would be the first day of the week, a Sunday. It was Feast of Firstfruits.

These are the journeys of the children of Israel, which went forth out of the land of Egypt with their armies under the hand of Moses and Aaron. And Moses wrote their goings out according to their journeys by the commandment of the LORD: and these are their journeys according to their goings out. And they departed from Rameses in the first month, on the fifteenth day of the first month; on the morrow after the passover the children of Israel went out with an high hand in the sight of all the Egyptians. For the Egyptians buried all their firstborn, which the LORD had smitten among them: upon their gods also the LORD executed judgments. And the children of Israel removed from Rameses, and pitched in Succoth. And they departed from Succoth, and pitched in Etham, which is in the edge of the

63

wilderness. And they removed from Etham, and turned again unto Pihahiroth, which is before Baalzephon: and they pitched before Migdol. And they departed from before Pihahiroth, and passed through the midst of the sea into the wilderness, and went three days' journey in the wilderness of Etham, and pitched in Marah. (Numbers 33:1-8)

Passover was on a full moon the 14th day of the month Nisan. That night the Angel of the Lord smote every firstborn in the land. Pharaoh's son was among the dead. The next morning Pharaoh called for Moses and Aaron and told them to take the Hebrews, their cattle, and all they owned and leave Egypt. They left Egypt in haste on the 15th. That night they camped in Succoth. The next day they camped at Ethan, and on the evening which began the 17th, they were at Migdol. The next day which is still the 17th of Nisan, they would cross over the Red Sea. Pharaoh and his army would be swallowed up trying to cross. They did not have the blood applied. You cannot get into the assembly of God without the blood. The time-line of days and nights will not make sense to you unless you understand that a day starts at 6:00 PM (or sundown) in Israel. In other words, at 6:00 PM Saturday night in Israel it becomes Sunday. It can be a little confusing to us here in America since our day starts at midnight.

Passover is figurative of our salvation. The Feast of Unleavened Bread begins the evening of Passover and is figurative of our getting sin out of our lives. On the Feast of Firstfruits we cross over into the congregation by way of baptism in the Red Sea. This places us in an atmosphere where we can be around God's people and receive training and fellowship and encouragement.

6. The Feast of Pentecost is the place in our life where we begin to feed on the word of God.

When the Israelites crossed the Red Sea on the 17th of Nisan, they journeyed south to Mount Sinai. They would be camped there for some time while building the tabernacle. Later, Moses went up to the mountain to get the word of God, the Ten Commandments. Moses was on the mountain with God for forty days. While he was there, the people grew impatient and fashioned a golden calf and began to worship it. Many of the people fornicated and were drunken and rebellious. It is a sad story as we see in the following passage:

Exodus 32:*1 And when the people saw that Moses delayed to come down out of the mount, the people gathered themselves together unto Aaron, and said unto him, Up, make us gods, which shall go before us; for as for this Moses, the man that brought us up out of the land of Egypt, we wot not what is become of him.*

2 And Aaron said unto them, Break off the golden earrings, which are in the ears of your wives, of your sons, and of your daughters, and bring them unto me.

3 And all the people brake off the golden earrings which were in their ears, and brought them unto Aaron.

4 And he received them at their hand, and fashioned it with a graving tool, after he had made it a molten calf: and they said, These be thy gods, O Israel, which brought thee up out of the land of Egypt.

5 And when Aaron saw it, he built an altar before it; and Aaron made proclamation, and said, <u>To morrow is a feast to the LORD</u>.

6 And they rose up early on the morrow, and offered burnt offerings, and brought peace offerings; and the people sat down to eat and to drink, and rose up to play.

7 And the LORD said unto Moses, Go, get thee down; for thy people, which thou broughtest out of the land of Egypt, have corrupted themselves:

8 They have turned aside quickly out of the way which I commanded them: they have made them a molten calf, and have worshipped it, and have sacrificed thereunto, and said, These be thy gods, O Israel, which have brought thee up out of the land of Egypt.

In verse 5 we see that there is a feast on the morrow. I believe it is a reference to the Feast of Pentecost.

And Moses turned, and went down from the mount, and the two tables of the testimony were in his hand: the tables were written on both their sides; on the one side and on the other were they written. And the tables were the work of God, and the writing was the writing of God, graven upon the tables. And when Joshua heard the noise of the people as they shouted, he said unto Moses, There is a noise of war in the camp. And he said, It is not the voice of them that shout for mastery, neither is it the voice of them that cry for being overcome: but the noise of them that sing do I hear. And it came to pass, as soon as he came nigh unto the camp, that he saw the calf, and the dancing: and Moses' anger waxed hot, and he cast the tables out of his hands, and brake them beneath the mount. And he took the calf which they had made, and burnt it in the fire, and ground it to powder, and strawed it upon the water, and made the children of Israel drink of it. (Exodus 32:15-20)

Later, Moses instructed the people to draw swords against those who would not repent.

And when Moses saw that the people were naked; (for Aaron had made them naked unto their shame among their enemies:) Then Moses stood in the gate of the camp, and said, Who is on the LORD'S side? let him come unto me. And all the sons of Levi gathered themselves together unto him.

And he said unto them, Thus saith the LORD God of Israel, Put every man his sword by his side, and go in and out from gate to gate throughout the camp, and slay every man his brother, and every man his companion, and every man his neighbour. And the children of Levi did according to the word of Moses: and there fell of the people that day about three thousand men. For Moses had said, Consecrate yourselves to day to the LORD, even every man upon his son, and upon his brother; that he may bestow upon you a blessing this day. (Exodus 32:25-29)

What a sad turn of events as about 3000 men lose their lives over this sin in the congregation. About 1500 years later, on the last Pentecost in Acts 2, about 3000 were added to the church. The lesson is this: *"The law killeth, but the Spirit giveth life."*

7. The last stage of the journey is the crossing of the Jordan River where we live the victorious life as a Spirit-filled Christian.

Because of their sin and faithlessness, they had to wait forty years before crossing the Jordan River. They all died in the wilderness. The wilderness is where most Christians live. Most believers will never cross the Jordan River and enter into that joyous life of living by faith. This story certainly teaches us that. Only Joshua and Caleb crossed over, they... and those who were under 18 years of age at the time of the Red Sea crossing.

Observations

1. You can not skip any of these stages of the journey.
2. Each stage has a major river to cross. Each stage has an obstacle that must be faced.
3. The promised land is the will of God for all believers.
4. There is a divine order of things taught in this lesson.
5. God commands us to be going forward.

My friend, have you discovered where you are living in this time-line? Are you still in Egypt living a worldly life? Are you on the mountain getting the word of God in you? Are you wandering in the wilderness? Or maybe you are one of the few who made it across the Jordan and are living by faith. The important thing is to discover where you are and admit to yourself that you have not arrived. Decide to shake the dust off yourself and go forward.

The Theme Throughout the Entire Bible is that God Wants to Fellowship with Man

PROPHETIC VIEW OF THE SEVEN FEASTS
Chapter 7

In the Bible we learn that Israel had seven major feasts. As you will see, it is amazing how these feasts are symbolic of future events. We are going to take a prophetic look at these seven feasts. We have already studied the passage in Leviticus 23 that lists all seven. Below is a list of the feasts:

THE SEVEN FEASTS
Leviticus 23

1. Feast of Passover .... Nisan 10th-14th (Our March or April)

2. Feast of Unleavened bread....Nisan 15th-21st, 7 days

3. Feast of Firstfruits....First day of week after Passover

4. Feast of Pentecost....50 days after Firstfruits

FOUR MONTH GAP HERE

5. Feast of Trumpets.... 1st day of seventh month

6. Feast of Day of Atonement.... 10th day of seventh month

7. Feast of Tabernacles.... 15th day of seventh month

The seven feasts take place during the first seven months of the Jewish year. Seven is God's number of completion. I believe there will be seven thousand years of human history. There were six days of creation and God rested on the seventh day. *But, beloved, be not ignorant of this one thing, that one day is with the Lord as a thousand years, and a thousand years as one day.* (2 Peter 3:8)

The first four feasts symbolize events that have already taken place. The last three take place in the fall and are symbolic of events yet to come. Christ fulfilled the first four feasts right to the exact day. Isn't that amazing? Will the last three be fulfilled on their exact day? It is possible, and in fact very probable since we know He is a God of order. As you can see in the list above, there was a four-month gap where the people did not come together for any feasts. The reason for this is they were working in the fields preparing a harvest. The Feast of Trumpets begins the three fall feasts and it occurs with the blowing of the trumpet. The trumpet begins the feast and the people assemble to bring in the harvest. That is interesting in light of the rapture being a harvest of souls, is not it?

Now let us look at these seven feasts and see how they apply to us in the light of prophecy. **These seven feasts are the Bible's built-in prophetic calendar.** If you will get an understanding of them it will greatly enlighten your view of future events.

On the Feast of Passover, exactly at the right time, Christ our Passover Lamb (I Corinthians 5:7) went to the cross and paid in full the sin debt of the world. This took place 483 years, (69 weeks) after the command to build the wall in Nehemiah as explained in the book of Daniel. You see, nobody knew the date of the birth of Christ, but anyone who studied Daniel knew exactly when Messiah would be cut off. The birth of Christ was a mystery revealed only to Joseph and Mary and a few others. I do not believe even Satan knew who Christ was until John baptized Him. The wise men did not show up until almost two years after Jesus was born. Christmas came from the traditions of Rome and has thrown us off for centuries. The New Testament did not start at the birth of Christ, but at the death of Christ. Satan was probably watching John the Baptist, thinking he was the Messiah. Do you have any other explanation for the fact that John was filled with the Holy Ghost from his mother's womb? It may be that it was for the purpose of throwing off the Devil! John may have been a decoy. On what we call "Palm Sunday" Christ rode into Jerusalem on a donkey and presented Himself to the people as a perfect sacrificial lamb. He fulfilled all the requirements of Exodus 12. The people watched Him for four days just as they were instructed to do in Exodus 12. After four days, the Lamb of God was put on a cross. He shed His blood and died. He was put in the tomb by 6:00 P.M. which is the beginning of the next day, which would be Thursday. (Remember their day ends at sundown rather than midnight like ours.) This was the beginning of the next feast, Unleavened Bread. He proved He was sinless and no leaven of corruption was found in His body. Christ rose on the exact day of the Feast of Firstfruits which began on Sunday, Nisan the 17th. This happened at 6:00 P.M. Saturday night which is Sunday on their clock. Christ was in the tomb from 6:00 P.M. Wednesday to 6:00 P.M. Saturday night which is the beginning of Sunday. He was in the grave three days and three nights and rose on the first day of the week just as the Bible said He would. The fourth feast is Pentecost which is fifty days after Feast of Firstfruits. We see what happened in Acts Chapter 2. Christ empowered His church to go out and labor on a harvest. That is what this feast was all about. It was to encourage the people concerning the harvest. Christ empowered His church to go out and plant the seed of the word of God to get a harvest of souls, to get a BRIDE for Jesus Christ! Do you see how each of these first four feasts were fulfilled right to the exact day and that they all picture something that has already happened? Now hang on to your seat! There are three more feasts, and these picture future events that have

71

not yet been fulfilled. The next event on God's calendar is the rapture. What does the Bible say about the rapture? Something about trumpets right? I Thessalonians 4:15-18, Revelation 4:1 and I Corinthians 15:52 all speak of the rapture occurring with the sound of a trumpet. The Feast of Trumpets is prophetic of the rapture.

1 Thessalonians 4:15-18 For this we say unto you by the word of the Lord, that we which are alive and remain unto the coming of the Lord shall not prevent them which are asleep. For the Lord himself shall descend from heaven with a shout, with the voice of the archangel, and with the trump of God: and the dead in Christ shall rise first: Then we which are alive and remain shall be caught up together with them in the clouds, to meet the Lord in the air: and so shall we ever be with the Lord. Wherefore comfort one another with these words.

Revelation 4:1 After this I looked, and, behold, a door was opened in heaven: and the first voice which I heard was as it were of a trumpet talking with me; which said, Come up hither, and I will shew thee things which must be hereafter.

1 Corinthians 15:52
In a moment, in the twinkling of an eye, at the last trump: for the trumpet shall sound, and the dead shall be raised incorruptible, and we shall be changed.

There are 29 days in the month Elul which is the month right before Tishri. The Jews would blow a trumpet each of these 29 days looking forward to the "last trump" which is the announcement of the Feast of Trumpets on Tishri 1. The Jews call the Feast of Trumpets "Rosh Hashanah."

Why Feast of Trumpets is prophetic of the Rapture

1. It is the next feast of the seven awaiting fulfillment, just as the rapture is the next event on God's time table.
2. It is the one feast that no man knows the day or hour that

72

it begins. Feast of Trumpets is the only feast that begins on the new moon which is the first day of the month. This feast did not begin until the representatives of the temple, usually two men who were sent to the hillside, had actually seen the sliver of the new moon in the sky and reported back to the High Priest. It was then that the trumpet would be blown and the feast would officially begin.

3. It is the feast that fits the description of the rapture with the blowing of trumpets.

4. It is the beginning of fruit harvest. The rapture is a harvest of the souls of men.

In Bible days, the trumpet was blown to assemble the people. They would blow trumpets on the Feast of Trumpets to assemble the people at the harvest time. Now the first four feasts all happened on the exact day of the feasts. Does that mean the rapture will happen on Feast of Trumpets? I do not know, but it could. It sure makes logical sense doesn't it? However, God's people are to be looking for Him every day. Trumpets occurs at the new moon, which is the first day of the seventh month which is Tishri. (It would be in our months of Sept. or Oct.) This begins a two day feast.

After the Feast of Trumpets is the Day of Atonement. This is the sixth feast. The Jews call it Yom Kippur. It is a most holy day for the Jews. It was the one time of year that the High Priest could enter the Holy of Holies and offer the sacrifice for the nation. It was at this time that Zachariah was visited by an angel who announced that Elizabeth was going to have a son, and he was to name him John. I believe this sixth feast is prophetic of the Second Coming of Christ at the end of the Tribulation. This is where Christ stands on the Mountain of Olives as was prophesied in Acts 1:11-12, when Christ comes back as King of Kings and Lord of Lords!

Which also said, Ye men of Galilee, why stand ye gazing up into heaven? this same Jesus, which is taken up from you into heaven, shall so come in like manner as ye have seen him go into heaven. Then returned they unto Jerusalem from the mount called Olivet, which is from Jerusalem a Sabbath day's journey.

Jesus became our High Priest when the veil was rent.

Hebrews 3:1 Wherefore, holy brethren, partakers of the heavenly calling, consider the Apostle and High Priest of our profession, Christ Jesus;

Hebrews 4:14-16 Seeing then that we have a great high priest, that is passed into the heavens, Jesus the Son of God, let us hold fast our profession. For we have not an high priest which cannot be touched with the feeling of our infirmities; but was in all points tempted like as we are, yet without sin. Let us therefore come boldly unto the throne of grace, that we may obtain mercy, and find grace to help in time of need.

Hebrews 6:20 Whither the forerunner is for us entered, even Jesus, made an high priest for ever after the order of Melchisedec.

The last feast is called Tabernacles. The people would gather and dwell in tents, some called booths. It is five days after Atonement. They would dwell there for seven days. It was a time of rest after the harvest. It is a type of the 1000-year Sabbath rest called the Millennium. Shortly after returning to the Mountain of Olives with the title deed to planet earth in His hand; Christ will set up His kingdom and rule for 1000 years. These last three feasts all take place in the seventh month, which is our September or October. It is harvest time; it is in the Fall. The Lord is coming back. The seven feasts give us a very intimate prophetic look at the future events. We are to be watching for Him. May we be found faithful when He comes for us!

GOD'S FINAL JUBILEE
Chapter 8

And thou shalt number seven sabbaths of years unto thee, seven times seven years; and the space of the seven sabbaths of years shall be unto thee forty and nine years. Then shalt thou cause the trumpet of the jubile to sound on the tenth day of the seventh month, in the day of atonement shall ye make the trumpet sound throughout all your land. And ye shall hallow the fiftieth year, and proclaim liberty throughout all the land unto all the inhabitants thereof: it shall be a jubile unto you; and ye shall return every man unto his possession, and ye shall return every man unto his family. A jubile shall that fiftieth year be unto you: ye shall not sow, neither reap that which groweth of itself in it, nor gather the grapes in it of thy vine undressed. For it is the jubile; it shall be holy unto you: ye shall eat the increase thereof out of the field. In the year of this jubile ye shall return every man unto his possession. (Leviticus 25:8-13)

Apart from the seven feasts, nothing will do more for your understanding of prophecy than the information about the Jubilee in this chapter. Like me, I suspect that many of you reading this book have not been taught much about the Jubilee. I listed some verses from Leviticus 25, but actually the whole of Chapter 25 is about the Jubilee. Leviticus 25:1-7 explains the Sabbath of the land. Amazing isn't it? We will come back to that, but everything seems to point towards the seventh day which is the Sabbath. In Genesis 1, God created everything in six days and rested on the seventh. Those seven days represent seven thousand years of history. The world will go for six thousand years and then rest for a thousand years. It is called the Millennium. God will dwell with man. That is and was the plan from the beginning. God wants to dwell with man. God wants to tabernacle with man. That is what the seventh feast is all about. Feast of Tabernacles is about God and man dwelling together in sweet fellowship. The word "Tabernacle" means to dwell with. **The seven feasts are so important to understanding it all. They are the key that unlocks the door to prophecy. They are God's prophetic calendar.** There are seven feasts described in Leviticus 23. These seven feasts take place within the first seven months of the Jewish year, from Nisan to Tishri. There is that seven again. God's special number, the number of completion. On Feast of Passover, Christ went to the cross and died. He was the Passover Lamb. He paid our sin debt during the full moon on Passover, the 14th of Nisan. Jesus lay in the grave on the second feast, Feast of Unleavened Bread, proving there was no leaven or sin in His body. On Feast of Firstfruits Christ rose from the grave victorious over sin and death. On Feast of Pentecost, the fourth feast, Christ empowered the church in Acts Chapter 2 to sow the seed of the word of God to get a bride for Jesus Christ. Each of these four feast were fulfilled right to the day! Is that significant? I certainly think so.

Now there are three feasts left that have not yet been fulfilled. They are fall feasts and all take place in the seventh month, the month Tishri. Tishri is in late September or early October on our solar calendar. The next feast is Trumpets. The Jews call it Rosh Hashanah. It is on the new moon which is the first day of their month. It is also their New Years Day. This feast will be fulfilled when the trumpet blows and we are caught up in the clouds to be with the Lord. Will it happen on the actual Feast of Trumpets on the Jewish calendar? There is no way to know. The calendar has been messed with. The Jewish calendar may not be right either. Seven years later Jesus will come back on the Feast of Day of Atonement to end the battle of Armageddon and put away the Antichrist. It happens in Revelation 19:11 and the saints will come back with him. In fact you and I will be with Him. It will be a great day! Atonement is on the 10th of Tishri. Five days later is the seventh feast which is Tabernacles and will be fulfilled by the setting up of the Kingdom of our Lord Jesus Christ and the beginning of the 1000 year reign we call the millennium. It is the seventh day of the creative week in Genesis 1, and it is the Lord's Sabbath rest. This is the whole history of the world in a nut shell. God created man to fellowship with, to tabernacle with. Man sinned and broke that fellowship. Passover, Unleavened Bread, and Firstfruits are God's plan to redeem man and get back this fellowship. Pentecost is Christ empowering the church to go out and get people saved which brings in more folks to fellowship with God. The Feast of Trumpets is the great harvest of souls. It is in the fall, and it is the harvest time. It is the Bridegroom coming for His bride! We then have a seven-day wedding celebration in Heaven, while the Tribulation is going on down here on the earth. Then we come back with the Bridegroom on White horses on Atonement and He sets up the 1000 year Kingdom Age where we will live and reign with the Lord.

Now, back to our subject at hand. There is a Jubilee coming. The Jubilee is a Sabbath. There are several Sabbaths in the Bible. **We are not under the Sabbath in the New Testament Age.** As we said earlier, it was a shadow of Christ and our resting in Him for salvation. *Let no man therefore judge you in meat, or in drink, or in respect of an holyday, or of the new moon, or of the sabbath days: Which are a shadow of things to come; but the body is of Christ. (Colossians 2:16-17)*

After Christ died on the cross, the veil of the temple was rent in two. The Old Testament ended and the New

Covenant began. *And, behold, the veil of the temple was rent in twain from the top to the bottom; and the earth did quake, and the rocks rent; Matthew 27:51*

Now the believers would assemble on the first day of the week instead of the sixth day. I believe this was just another sign from God that the Old Testament had ended.

John 20:19 Then the same day at evening, being the <u>first day of the week</u>, when the doors were shut where the disciples were assembled for fear of the Jews, came Jesus and stood in the midst, and saith unto them, Peace be unto you.

Acts 20:7 And upon the <u>first day of the week</u>, when the disciples came together to break bread, Paul preached unto them, ready to depart on the morrow; and continued his speech until midnight.

1 Corinthians 16:2 Upon the <u>first day of the week </u>let every one of you lay by him in store, as God hath prospered him, that there be no gatherings when I come.

God did not put away the Old Testament laws; He fulfilled them. Do you understand the difference? Christ was what all the lambs and sacrifices had represented. He was the Lamb, He fulfilled what they pictured. They are still wonderful principles and lessons for us, but we are not under the ceremonial laws of the Old Testament. *Matthew 5:17 Think not that I am come to destroy the law, or the prophets: I am not come to destroy, but to fulfil.*

Before we move on to the Jubilee, let me give you <u>an illustration that folks have said was helpful in understanding why we do not keep the Sabbath or the other ceremonial laws today.</u> Imagine that you come to a prophecy conference and meet me in person and I show you a photo of my family. That would be fine, but imagine if my family is sitting just a few feet away! That would be a little strange wouldn't it? Wouldn't it be better to just introduce you to them in person?

You see, keeping a Sabbath or killing a lamb today would be foolish. Those were figures and types to point us to the Christ who was to come. Since Christ has come those things have been fulfilled and we now can see clearly. We do not need the types and figures anymore, we have the real thing! Trying to go back under the ceremonial law would be like showing your friends a photo of your family who are sitting right beside you. It would make no sense at all. If you are going to place yourself under the Sabbath, why do you not also kill a Passover lamb each year? If you want to be back under the ceremonial law, why not keep ALL of it? Do you know that even the Jews stopped killing lambs two-thousand years ago? Even the Jews, subconsciously, know that Jesus Christ fulfilled that practice.

Now, I said all that because we are going to look at some Sabbaths. In order for you to fully appreciate what the Jubilee is, we need to review some principles about the Sabbath. We will get to the Jubilee shortly, but follow closely as we look at the following concerning God's Sabbath. <u>The seventh creative day in Genesis Chapter 1 was a Sabbath</u>. God rested on the seventh day. He set a precedent there. All through the Bible the Sabbath is important to God. The seventy-year captivity of the children of Israel in Babylon was in fact God's judgment against them for not honoring the Sabbath. We see how serious God is about the Sabbath in these Scriptures:

And them that had escaped from the sword carried he away to Babylon; where they were servants to him and his sons until the reign of the kingdom of Persia: To fulfil the word of the LORD by the mouth of Jeremiah, until the land had enjoyed her sabbaths: for as long as she lay desolate she kept sabbath, to fulfil threescore and ten years.
(2 Chronicles 36:20-21)

We are no longer under Old Testament ceremonial law,

but there are many figurative and prophetic lessons concerning it. There are three Sabbaths I want you to see.

1. The <u>seventh day</u> of the week is a Sabbath.

Remember the sabbath day, to keep it holy. Six days shalt thou labour, and do all thy work: But the seventh day is the sabbath of the LORD thy God: in it thou shalt not do any work, thou, nor thy son, nor thy daughter, thy manservant, nor thy maidservant, nor thy cattle, nor thy stranger that is within thy gates: For in six days the LORD made heaven and earth, the sea, and all that in them is, and rested the seventh day: wherefore the LORD blessed the sabbath day, and hallowed it. (Exodus 20:8-11)

This is a Sabbath for man. It is a day for man to rest from all his labors. It is also figurative. For instance, in the book of Numbers a man was put to death for picking up sticks on the Sabbath. The Sabbath is a picture of resting in Christ for our salvation. Picking up sticks was a type of working and not trusting fully in Messiah for salvation. If you truly want to place yourself under the Old Testament Sabbath and keep the Sabbath in a scriptural manner, you can not even pick up sticks for you fire, or cook or do any labor. You can not even travel. And at least keep it at the right time. Sabbath is from sundown Friday evening to sundown Saturday evening. There certainly is a principle taught here that man needs to rest from his labor once each week, but man is no longer under the Sabbath of the law.

2. The <u>seventh year</u> is a Sabbath for the land.

Speak unto the children of Israel, and say unto them, When ye come into the land which I give you, then shall the land keep a sabbath unto the LORD. Six years thou shalt sow thy field, and six years thou shalt prune thy vineyard, and gather in the fruit thereof; But in the seventh year shall be a sabbath of rest unto the land, a sabbath for the LORD: thou shalt neither sow thy field, nor prune thy vineyard. (Lev 25:2-4)

80

This was God's plan for restoring the land. Over time, the nutrients will become depleted from the soil. God ordained that in the sixth year they would harvest twice the crop. In the seventh year they would let the land rest. They would live off the double harvest the year before. The people had to trust in the Lord to operate under His system. It also was a time that the servants as well as the animals would rest. This is the Sabbath that Israel had broken that brought about the seventy-year captivity as we saw in 2 Chronicles 36:20-21 earlier.

3. The 49th year is a Sabbath called the Jubilee.

And thou shalt number seven sabbaths of years unto thee, seven times seven years; and the space of the seven sabbaths of years shall be unto thee forty and nine years. Then shalt thou cause the trumpet of the jubile to sound on the tenth day of the seventh month, in the day of atonement shall ye make the trumpet sound throughout all your land.
(Leviticus 25:8-9)

Every seventh day is a Sabbath for man to rest. Every seventh year was a Sabbath for the land to rest. After the 49th year (7X7 years) it was a Jubilee. Not only was it a rest for the land, but it was a proclamation of liberty throughout the land. In that day a trumpet was sounded and the whole 50th year was proclaimed as a Jubilee. Several things happened at the Jubilee. These are very prophetic of things to come so don't miss it.

1. All property went back to the original owner on the Jubilee.

Leviticus 25:13 This is how the Lord kept the land in the possession of the original 12 tribes as appointed under Joshua. Do not miss what I am saying here. Remember, this is a prophecy book and this chapter deals with the final Jubilee. Put your thinking cap on and you are going to see something you may have never noticed before. What I am

81

about to give you is the very heart and soul of this book! According to Leviticus Chapter 25 the Jubilee is begun at the end of the 49th year on the Day of Atonement which is the sixth feast! *Then shalt thou cause the trumpet of the jubile to sound on the tenth day of the seventh month, in the day of atonement shall ye make the trumpet sound throughout all your land.* *(Leviticus 25:9)*

Every 49 years on the Day of Atonement, the trumpet is sounded and the whole 50th year is a Jubilee year. Has it hit you yet? Prophetically, the Day of Atonement is the day that Christ comes back to the earth on the white horse at the end of the Tribulation and puts down the Antichrist and liberates the earth.

And I saw heaven opened, and behold a white horse; and he that sat upon him was called Faithful and True, and in righteousness he doth judge and make war. His eyes were as a flame of fire, and on his head were many crowns; and he had a name written, that no man knew, but he himself. And he was clothed with a vesture dipped in blood: and his name is called The Word of God. And the armies which were in heaven followed him upon white horses, clothed in fine linen, white and clean. And out of his mouth goeth a sharp sword, that with it he should smite the nations: and he shall rule them with a rod of iron: and he treadeth the winepress of the fierceness and wrath of Almighty God. And he hath on his vesture and on his thigh a name written, KING OF KINGS, AND LORD OF LORDS. *(Revelation 19:11-16)*

Since Christ is the original owner of the earth, can you see the significance of the Jubilee in regards to the second coming? *The land shall not be sold for ever: for the land is mine; for ye are strangers and sojourners with me.* *(Leviticus 25:23)*

I believe Christ will fulfill not only the Day of

Atonement, but the Jubilee as well and will do so on the very same day!

All property goes back to the original owner every 50 years. If you sold your property the year before, it now belongs to you again. Obviously, anyone buying property understood this and would not have paid much for it. Basically they were leasing the property. This is God's plan. This is how God set it up. There are many interesting details about the Jubilee in regards to buying and selling property, but we will not be able to get into it in great detail in this book.

2. All debt was forgiven on the Jubilee.

Wow, how do you like that? If you were in debt, it was forgiven on the day of Jubilee. This gave all men a fresh start at life. It also kept the lenders in check. For instance, if the Jubilee is just a few months or years away, would you be giving a ten year loan to someone? So the Jubilee even had a way of keeping debt under control.

3. All bond slaves were set free on the Jubilee.

If you had gone into debt and sold yourself as a bond slave to pay your debt, you and your family would go free at the Jubilee. This was God's plan.

Now, these things are a prophetic picture of what Jesus has done for the sinner, and what He is coming to do at His second coming. When we trust Christ for salvation, He sets us free from the penalty and payment of sin that we owe. He wipes the slate clean! Liberty is achieved. We were bond servants and slaves to sin but now we are set free. The Jubilee is a type of this, but there is more. You see, since the earth was also cursed when man sinned, it too must be redeemed. This will happen during the Tribulation. This is what the seven-sealed book in Revelation 5 is all about. Christ is the Kinsman Redeemer and will redeem the earth during the Tribulation. This is explained in detail in the next chapter. **At the final day when Christ comes back to the earth on the Day of Atonement, I believe it will be a Jubilee year and Christ will have the seven-sealed book in His hand and will stand on the Mountain of Olives and will proclaim liberty and will take back possession of the earth.** That is what the Jubilee does right? All property goes back to the original owner at the Jubilee. Hey, the Lord is the original owner of the earth! (Psalms 24:1) *The earth is the LORD'S, and the fulness thereof; the world, and they that dwell therein.*

Let me review what we have discussed. In Old Testament times, man was to keep the Sabbath every seventh day. It was a day of rest; it was for man. Every seventh year there was a Sabbath for the land. This gave the land rest as well as a rest for the servants and animals. The Jubilee was every 49th year. Every 49 years, (7 X 7 years) a Jubilee was proclaimed and celebrated for the entire 50th year. All property went back to the original owner. All debt was forgiven and all bond servants went free. This Jubilee happens to occur every 49th year on the sixth feast which is the Day of Atonement. This is the very feast that is prophetic of Christ coming back to the earth at the end of the Tribulation to set up the Kingdom Age. *Then shalt thou cause the trumpet of the jubile to sound on the tenth day of the seventh month, <u>in the day of atonement </u>shall ye make the trumpet sound throughout all your land. (Leviticus 25:9)*

Summary

Christ paid our sin debt on Passover. He lay in the grave during Unleavened Bread proving there was no leaven or sin in His body. Christ rose victorious over death and the grave on the Feast of Firstfruits. On Pentecost He empowered the church to go out and till the ground, plant, water, and get a crop in the ground. At the end of the 2000 year church age

84

He comes back on Feast of Trumpets to reap the harvest of souls at what we call the rapture. He comes as a Bridegroom to get His bride. When He takes us out of here, God again deals with Israel while the church is spending seven years at a wedding celebration. At the end of the seven years we come back with the Bridegroom at the end of the Tribulation to end the battle of Armageddon. Christ stands on the Mountain of Olives in fulfillment of the sixth feast, the Day of Atonement. It also happens to be a Jubilee year. In fact, it is the 70th Jubilee since it was given to Moses in 1500 B.C. Does that give you a reason to shout? Christ has the Seven-Sealed Book which is the title deed to planet earth in His hand and liberty is proclaimed through out the land. Satan is cast into the bottomless pit and the Kingdom Age begins on the seventh feast which is Feast of Tabernacles. God and man will "dwell together" for a 1000 years!

3 reasons the second coming of the Lord is a Jubilee:

1. Because of the prophetic meaning of the Jubilee.
Everything God set up has a purpose and a meaning. The Jubilee fits the second coming of Christ perfectly! At the Jubilee all debt is forgiven, all bond servants are made free, and all property goes back to the original owner. This is all fulfilled completely at the return of the Lord.

2. Because we are coming up on the 70th Jubilee.
There is that number seven again. Moses was given the instructions about the Jubilee approximately 1500 B.C. We will have 2000 years in the New Testament Age. That makes 3500 years total. Each Jubilee cycle is 50 years total. If you divide 3500 by 50 you get 70 Jubilees. I realize Israel has not kept the Jubilee in hundreds of years, but I have no doubt that the Lord has kept up with it. After all, it is a Sabbath, right? God kept up with the Sabbaths that the children of

Israel profaned and gave them seventy years of captivity in Babylon as a result of it. The next Jubilee on the near horizon is the 70th Jubilee. Do you think that might be significant? I certainly think it is.

3. We are coming up on the 120th Jubilee.

From the time of Adam until now is 120 Jubilee periods of 50 years each. I realize that the Jubilee did not officially start until 1500 B.C. However, did you know that if you go back and start at Genesis 1 and count until the end of the 2000th year of the New Testament you get 6000 years? If you divide 6000 by 50 you get 120 Jubilee years. Is that interesting? Consider this passage of Scripture in light of that.

And it came to pass, when men began to multiply on the face of the earth, and daughters were born unto them, That the sons of God saw the daughters of men that they were fair; and they took them wives of all which they chose. And the LORD said, My spirit shall not always strive with man, for that he also is flesh: yet his days shall be an hundred and twenty years. There were giants in the earth in those days; and also after that, when the sons of God came in unto the daughters of men, and they bare children to them, the same became mighty men which were of old, men of renown. (Genesis 6:1-4)

We are not going to get into the discussion of who the sons of God were. What I do want you to look at is the verse I underlined above. Notice that God says man's days shall be 120 years. Most folks think that is talking about the years Noah spent building the ark. That is what I believed for many years. Problem with that is it is not accurate. Noah spent no more than 100 years building the ark. We see here that Noah was 500 years of age when his children began to be born. *And Noah was five hundred years old: and Noah begat Shem, Ham, and Japheth.* (Genesis 5:32*)*

These are the generations of Noah: Noah was a just man and perfect in his generations, and Noah walked with God. And <u>*Noah begat three sons, Shem, Ham, and Japheth.*</u> *The earth also was corrupt before God, and the earth was filled with violence. And God looked upon the earth, and, behold, it was corrupt; for all flesh had corrupted his way upon the earth. And God said unto Noah, The end of all flesh is come before me; for the earth is filled with violence through them; and, behold, I will destroy them with the earth.* <u>*Make thee an ark of gopher wood;*</u> *rooms shalt thou make in the ark, and shalt pitch it within and without with pitch.* (Genesis 6:9-14)

The command to build the ark was obviously given AFTER Noah's three sons were born.

(Genesis 7:6) *And* <u>*Noah was six hundred years old*</u> *when the flood of waters was upon the earth.* It is plain that Noah was commanded to build the ark AFTER he was 500 years old and AFTER his three sons were born. Then we see that the rains began when Noah was 600 years old. That means Noah was 100 years or less building the ark.

Now, I pointed this out because we all have been given some wrong teaching on the 120 years in Genesis 6:3, and I want to give you a theory about what I believe God is telling us in the passage. It is my opinion that God is telling us that His Spirit is going to dwell with man upon the earth for 120 generations and I believe a generation is 50 years. 120 generations of 50 year periods would be 6000 years. If I am right about this, then God was saying that there will be 120 Jubilees making up 6000 years and then the end. My friend, the next Jubilee on the time clock of Heaven will be the 120th from Adam.

Jubilees From Genesis to Revelation

From creation to the end of the Tribulation is 6000 years. There are 120 Jubilees in a 6000 year period. I realize that the Jubilee did not officially start until 1500 BC with Moses, but as we discussed, according to Geneses 6:3 it appears that God established the Jubilee to mark the whole history of man. With that in mind, I want to show you some Jubilees in history that will add some notoriety to my theory.

1. The 40th Jubilee is the year 2000 B.C. and the beginning of the Hebrew people with the life of Abraham and the covenant God made with him. This is certainly figurative of the Jubilee. Abraham was a new beginning. He was the Father of the Hebrew race that would deliver them. The Jew would be free to have a special relationship with Jehovah God.

2. The 50th Jubilee is the year 1500 B.C. and is the year that Israel left Egypt in the Exodus. Since the Jubilee is of such importance, and is celebrated every 50th year, do you suppose there would be anything significant about the fiftieth Jubilee?

God instituted the 7 Feasts beginning with the Passover lamb and the death of the firstborn in Egypt. God led the children of Israel across the Red Sea on dry ground. This was around 1500 B.C. It was the biggest deliverance of slaves in the history of the world! Remember, that is what happens on the Jubilee. All slaves are set free and all debt is forgiven. Not only were they set free, but they left with the spoils of the Egyptians. They left debt free. How about that for a 50th Jubilee from the beginning of creation!

3. The 60th Jubilee is the year 1000 B.C. and is the building of Solomon's Temple.

This is 500 years after the Exodus from Egypt. After many battles and struggles, God calls Solomon to build the temple. They were at peace with the kingdoms around them.

In fact, kings and queens would come to visit Israel and bring gifts. Not only were they free but they were prosperous. God dwelt in the Temple. This certainly is figurative of a Jubilee.

4. The 70th Jubilee from creation is 500 B.C. and is deliverance from the seventy-year captivity in Babylon.

Once again, freedom from bondage and deliverance from debt. These are the days of Esther and Nehemiah and Ezra, and the restoring of the city and building of the wall.

5. The 80th Jubilee from creation is Calvary.

I guess there is nothing that needs to be said here. It should be obvious to all that deliverance and removal of the debt of sin can be seen here. Eight is the number of new beginnings.

So we see that the theory of the 120 Jubilees seems to fit throughout history. I am not saying they are necessarily right to the exact year in each case, but the principle is clearly seen. Besides, if you move the start of the New Testament to Calvary instead of the birth, it straightens out most of these issues.

When is God's final Jubilee

Obviously, the big question on the minds of everyone reading this chapter is, "When is this final Jubilee scheduled to happen?" I have to be honest and tell you that nobody knows for sure. I am not a date setter. The calendar is so messed up I do not think we can be sure of anything. The Israelites have not kept a Jubilee in over 2000 years. I have done some study on it and nobody is sure what year Israel kept its last Jubilee. The purpose of this book is not to set a date, but rather to get you to see we are close. However, let me share some possibilities with you about when the final Jubilee may occur.

There are many prophecy preachers and authors who

believe that 1967 was a Jubilee year. What happened in 1967 was a huge event. It was the famous Six-Day War in Israel. That is what history calls it. Israel became a nation in May of 1948 but they were much smaller then. They did not have the Golan Heights or the West Bank, but more importantly they did not posses Jerusalem. What is Israel without Jerusalem? During this famous Six-Day War, Israel was attacked by several Arab nations. If you do some research you will find many miraculous things took place and Israel defeated her enemies and won the Golan Heights, the West Bank area, and Jerusalem. The war lasted just six days.

Next would be the Yom Kippur War in the early 70's where they would acquire more land, but reclaiming Jerusalem in 1967 was an EPIC event! Because of the strange and miraculous things that happened, and the acquiring of the holy city of Jerusalem, some think it was a Jubilee year. It certainly fits the description of a Jubilee. The city of Jerusalem went back to the original owner, the Jews. Again, I am not saying that we know anything for sure, but what if it was a Jubilee? Is there anyway we can know? Well, I decided to go back 50 years and see if anything unusual happened concerning Israel in 1917. What I learned was shocking! In 1917 the Jews were still scattered. Jerusalem was inhabited by the Muslim Turks, who were a very fierce group of fighters. A British General named Allenby was ordered to force the Turks out and claim Jerusalem for Great Britain. What happens next is almost out of a children's fairytale but go research this yourself and see. What I am telling you actually happened. Printing was primitive in those days, as was the airplane. In fact, very few had ever seen an airplane. General Allenby came up with a plan. He decided to print some flyers and use airplanes to drop them over Jerusalem. The flyer said something like, "Get out of Jerusalem" and was signed Allenby. At least something like that written in Arabic. As I said, printing was primitive in those days. When the flyers arrived the name Allenby looked a lot like Allah in Arabic. In fact it is said to have been written as Alla Bay, which means Son of God in Arabic. When the Turks looked up and saw airplanes in the sky, something they may have never seen before, and began to read the flyers, they read it as follows: "Get out of Jerusalem now" signed Son of God. When General Allenby showed up days later with an army, they walked into Jerusalem and took it without firing one shot. What an amazing story! Now, does this have any characteristics of a Jubilee year?

Consider the following scenario

In 1917 on a Jubilee year, God gives Jerusalem to Great Britain, the Christian nation of the world at that time. Fifty years later on the 69th Jubilee, God gives Jerusalem back to those to whom it was promised, the Jews. In the next Jubilee, fifty years later in the fall of 2017, on God's 70th and final Jubilee, Jerusalem goes back to God who is the original owner. Again, I am not saying that 2017 is the final 70th Jubilee. I am saying it could be. If 1917 and 1967 were Jubilee years, then 2017 would also be a Jubilee year. It is interesting, is it not? I am sure you have already figured out that there are not enough years from now to the year 2017 to fit in the seven-year Tribulation. I have an answer for that in the chapter called 2520. For now, we will leave it there. Again, I want to caution you about trying to set a date. We have looked at some very exciting scenarios here, but they are just some possibilities. <u>The only thing we can be sure of is that the Lord is coming at the day appointed and no man knows the day or the hour.</u> It is near impossible to figure out the calendar. It has been messed with. I cannot be sure that 1917 or 1967 were Jubilee years. God has not told us they were; I am just speculating. What I do know is that the next Jubilee will be the 70th Jubilee. Now that is pretty significant if I may say so. I do not know when the Lord is coming for us. I believe it is soon. I believe it may be very soon. That is all I am saying.

Closing Observations

1. Jubilee is on Feast of Atonement every 49th year.
   It is celebrated the 50th year which makes it a complete 50 year period of years.
2. 50 Jubilees from Adam to Moses.
3. 70 Jubilees from Moses to Second Coming of Christ.
4. If 1967 was a Jubilee then 2017 would be a Jubilee.
5. The year 2018 is 70 years from Israel returning to their land in 1948.
6. Year 2017 is the year 5777 on Hebrew calendar. Even though their calendar has been manipulated on purpose to confuse Christians, I find that date interesting.
6. A man would ordinarily celebrate one Jubilee in his life time.

THE KINSMAN REDEEMER
Chapter 9

And I saw in the right hand of him that sat on the throne a book written within and on the backside, sealed with seven seals. And I saw a strong angel proclaiming with a loud voice, Who is worthy to open the book, and to loose the seals thereof? And no man in heaven, nor in earth, neither under the earth, was able to open the book, neither to look thereon. And I wept much, because no man was found worthy to open and to read the book, neither to look thereon. And one of the elders saith unto me, Weep not: behold, the Lion of the tribe of Juda, the Root of David, hath prevailed to open the book, and to loose the seven seals thereof. And I beheld, and, lo, in the midst of the throne and of the four beasts, and in the midst of the elders, stood a Lamb as it had been slain, having seven horns and seven eyes, which are the seven Spirits of God sent forth into all the earth. And he came and took the book out of the right hand of him that sat upon the throne. (Revelation 5:1-7)

In Revelation Chapter 1, Christ is seen in the midst of the seven golden candlesticks which are the churches. We see that these churches are His and He wants to have the pre-eminence in the church. In Chapters 2 and 3 we see the seven letters written to the seven churches. We clearly see that these seven churches have a prophetic meaning. We see that they represent the entire Church Age. **We are living in the final hours of the last Church Age right now!** Study the signs given in II Tim 3 and the attributes of the Laodicean church and it is obvious. In Chapter 4, the trump of God sounded and all believers were taken to Heaven.

Now this brings us to Revelation 5. You will be amazed at how our study of this chapter will go along with the Jubilee we discussed in the last chapter. Revelation Chapter 5 begins with a glimpse of One sitting on the throne with a book in His right hand. The One on the throne is the Father and the book is the Title Deed to the earth. Satan is the god of this world right now. Adam gave up the dominion of the earth. Part of the purpose of the Tribulation Period is to redeem the earth from the curse of sin. Way back in Genesis 3, we find that because of sin, a curse was placed upon the following three things: the Serpent, the ground (earth), and man. Man's soul was redeemed at Calvary (as soon as he trusts Christ), and his body shall be redeemed at the rapture when all the bodies of the saints shall be raised incorruptible and receive glorified bodies. (I Thessalonians 4:13-18 & I Corinthians 15:42-56) After the rapture, the earth shall be redeemed during the Tribulation, Daniel's 70th week. (See Daniel 9:24,12:4-9, and Isaiah 29:9-16)

In this chapter we are going to see that Jesus is our Kinsman Redeemer. We shall look at this in a moment, but let's first finish our summary of Revelation Chapter 5. Verse 2 asks, *"Who is worthy to open the book...?"* John weeps much because no man is found in Heaven or earth that is worthy to open the book. John is weeping for good reason, for if the book is not opened and the earth is not redeemed the church which is the bride of Christ cannot return to the earth for the 1000-year reign of Christ. Satan will be victorious. In verse 5, one of the twenty-four Elders, whom we saw in chapter 4, announces that someone has prevailed and is worthy to open the book. Hey, this is getting exciting now! *Revelation 5:5 And one of the elders saith unto me, Weep not: behold, the Lion of the tribe of Juda, the Root of David, hath prevailed to open the book, and to loose the seven seals thereof.* Of course, this is Jesus Christ Himself, and how interesting that the first time we see Jesus in John's vision of the rapture is here in Revelation 5:6 where we see Him in the midst of the elders and the throne. I believe that the twenty-four elders are figurative of all the saints gathered in Heaven at the rapture. We see the Trinity and also proof that it is the Father on the throne, and not Jesus. (We shall see Jesus on the throne in chapter 20.) Revelation 5:7 *And he came and took the book out of the right hand of him that sat upon the throne.* Jesus takes the book from the Father because He, and only He, meets the requirements of the Kinsman Redeemer. To fully understand Chapter 5 and this seven-sealed book which is the title deed to the earth, you need to understand the laws of the Kinsman redeemer as given to us in the Old Testament. Let me briefly explain this to you so that not only Revelation Chapter 5, but the whole Tribulation will make more sense to you. In fact, an understanding of this chapter is important to understanding the rest of the book of Revelation as well.

In Genesis 3, a curse came upon the serpent, man, and all creation. As I said above, man's soul was redeemed at Calvary, his body will be redeemed at the rapture. *Forasmuch as ye know that ye were not redeemed with corruptible things, as silver and gold, from your vain conversation received by tradition from your fathers; (1 Peter 1:18)*

Being born again, not of corruptible seed, but of incorruptible, by the word of God, which liveth and abideth for ever. (1 Peter 1:23)
And not only they, but ourselves also, which have the firstfruits of the Spirit, even we ourselves groan within ourselves, waiting for the adoption, to wit, the redemption of our body. (Romans 8:23)
We know that Satan is never going to be redeemed, but

what about the earth? Since we are coming back to this earth for 1000 years, it must be redeemed. This shall take place during the Tribulation, and is what the opening of the seven seals is all about. Romans 8:22 *For we know that the whole creation groaneth and travaileth in pain together until now.* This verse teaches that the whole world is in turmoil now because of the curse of God upon it. See a reference to this curse on the earth in the following passage.

And unto Adam he said, Because thou hast hearkened unto the voice of thy wife, and hast eaten of the tree, of which I commanded thee, saying, Thou shalt not eat of it: <u>cursed is the ground for thy sake</u>; in sorrow shalt thou eat of it all the days of thy life; Thorns also and thistles shall it bring forth to thee; and thou shalt eat the herb of the field; In the sweat of thy face shalt thou eat bread, till thou return unto the ground; for out of it wast thou taken: for dust thou art, and unto dust shalt thou return. (Genesis 3:17-19)

To understand the right of the Kinsman Redeemer, we need to look at some Old Testament principles.

Three things that could be redeemed in Bible days:
1. Widow- The brother of a deceased husband was to take his brother's wife as his own, as long as he could support her. In the book of Ruth we see that Boaz played the role of a kinsman redeemer and redeemed Naomi's land and also took Ruth for his wife. Did you know that the Lord Jesus is in the lineage of Boaz and Ruth? (Ruth 4)

Jesus fulfilled his role of Kinsman Redeemer by redeeming us. The church is the bride of Christ and was redeemed at Calvary. Do you see the prophetic picture there? *(Acts 20:28) Take heed therefore unto yourselves, and to all the flock, over the which the Holy Ghost hath made you overseers, to feed <u>the church</u> of God, which he*

96

hath <u>purchased with his own blood.</u>

(Revelation 21:9) And there came unto me one of the seven angels which had the seven vials full of the seven last plagues, and talked with me, saying, Come hither, I will shew thee the <u>bride, the Lamb's wife.</u>

Jesus, our Kinsman Redeemer, purchased us at a great price. We were lost in sin and sold ourselves into slavery. But praise the Lord we had a Kinsman who cared about us and purchased us at a great and terrible price!

2. Slave- One who could not pay his debts became a bond slave to his creditor for up to six years. We, too, were slaves to sin, but Romans 6:1-14 tells us we are redeemed and do not have to be a slave to sin! In fact, the new man, your spirit, that has been born again, cannot sin!

1 John 3:9 Whosoever is born of God doth not commit sin; for his seed remaineth in him: and he cannot sin, because he is born of God.

Our old man, the flesh, still sins. It is the old man that we struggle with. This flesh shall be redeemed at the rapture. We will get a glorified body when the trumpet sounds. So many go into false doctrine on this issue and claim that if we continue in sin, we are not saved. They will quote a verse like I John 3:9 to make their case. Yet the Bible clearly says in the same book, in *I John 1:8 If we say that we have no sin, we deceive ourselves, and the truth is not in us.*

Is this a contradiction in the Bible? No, it is speaking concerning the new man, the born again part, not the old man, the flesh. See *Ephesians 4:22-24 That ye put off concerning the former conversation the old man, which is corrupt according to the deceitful lusts; And be renewed in the spirit of your mind; And that ye put on the new man, which after God is created in righteousness and true holiness.* (see also Romans 6:6)

3. Land- Lost due to debt.

In the case of land, the Bible teaches the law of redemption concerning property or land. In the case of property, unlike a slave or a widow, when a person lost his property due to debt, a scroll was written up by the judges and ownership of the land was transferred to the creditor. It was kind of like a bank repossession or foreclosure in our day. However, this was not a permanent transfer in Old Testament days, as all land would go back to the original owner at the year of Jubilee. (We discussed this in the last chapter.) A document called a scroll would be written up. Inside that scroll would be the terms of redemption for the property. In other words, the cost of paying the debt on the property in order to get it back. This scroll would then be sealed until a kinsman comes in to redeem the land, or the debtor comes up with the money owed, or the day of Jubilee, which occurs every 49 years. The seal could only be broken by a person who meets the qualifications. This document is exactly what this scroll in Revelation 5 looks like! It too is sealed, and it too contains the terms of redemption of property. It is the title deed of all the earth which is right now owned and controlled by Satan. Adam was given dominion over the earth until he sinned and gave up that dominion to the Devil. During the Tribulation, the seven sealed book shall be opened and the terms of redemption of this sin cursed world shall be revealed and will be redeemed in full by Christ, the Kinsman Redeemer. The book of Leviticus 25:1-55 gives us three qualifications of the one who would redeem property. This explains why none were found worthy in Heaven and earth except the Lord Jesus. Let's look at these three requirements that Christ alone fulfilled:

Requirements of the Kinsman Redeemer

1. He must be a near kinsman of the person who lost the inheritance.

And one of the elders saith unto me, Weep not: behold, the Lion of the tribe of Juda, the Root of David, hath prevailed to open the book, and to loose the seven seals thereof. (Revelation 5:5)

Jesus fulfilled this role. He is of the right tribe and lineage. He was and is the only one who can!

2. He must be able to redeem it. He must have the financial ability to redeem it. Praise the Lord, *"He owns the cattle on a thousand hills...."* And He has the power and might to wrench it from the hands of Satan! You see, the devil is not going to let it go easily as the judges would; it must be taken by force by the Lord.

3. He must be willing to redeem the property.

The kinsman did not have to redeem the land if he did not choose to. (Ruth 4:1-12) But praise the Lord, Jesus is both willing and able to redeem the land. For examples of the Kinsman Redeemer, see Jeremiah 32:6-15, and the whole book of Ruth Chapters 1-4.

So you see, for 6000 years this old earth has been owned by Satan and is groaning and travailing under the curse of sin. We have gone through the whole Church Age in Revelation Chapters 2 and 3, the rapture has occurred in Chapter 4, and now we see the scroll in the right hand of the Father that contains the terms of the redemption of this world. Heaven and earth were searched for one who was worthy, one who met the three requirements of the kinsman redeemer, and none was found. Now do you understand why John was weeping? He knew the following:

1. If the book is not opened and the earth redeemed, all the Old Testament prophecies to be fulfilled in the Millennium

will be void.

2. All creation will remain under the curse. (Romans 8:22)
3. Israel will never be restored. (Romans 11:1-36)
4. Many Bible promises will be unfulfilled. (Matthew 5:18)

But praise the Lord, Jesus, our Kinsman Redeemer, meets the conditions and is both willing and able to open the book and loose the seals thereof. There is great rejoicing in Heaven over this event. In the next chapters, Revelation 6-19, we see the awful terms required for the redemption of this earth from the hands of Satan and from the curse of sin. The entire Tribulation takes place from Revelation 6-19. Read again Daniel 9:24 and realize that the Tribulation is not about Christians nor has it anything to do with the church. The Tribulation is all about the redemption of the earth to make an end of sin, to make reconciliation, and to anoint the Lord Jesus as King of Kings! It is also God dealing with Israel. God has one final week of years to deal with them and to bring in everlasting righteousness.

Seventy weeks are determined upon thy people and upon thy holy city, to finish the transgression, and to make an end of sins, and to make reconciliation for iniquity, and to bring in everlasting righteousness, and to seal up the vision and prophecy, and to anoint the most Holy. (Daniel 9:24)

Dear friends, this is such a great lesson! I trust that this has helped you in your understanding of the purpose and reason for end-time events.

OBSERVATIONS TO CONSIDER

1. Notice that there is weeping in Heaven.

Revelation 5:4 And I wept much, because no man was found worthy to open and to read the book, neither to look thereon.

You see, tears will not be wiped away until the end of the 1000 year reign of Christ and the Great White Throne judgment. (See Revelation 21:4)

I wonder if there are some moms who weep in Heaven over a wayward child. Maybe a child in Heaven weeps over a lost parent. I do not think I have ever heard anyone preach about tears in Heaven, yet it is clear that people can and do weep there. Tears are not wiped away until after the Great White Throne judgment after the 1000 year reign. I believe that this wiping away of our tears is also a wiping away of all memory of our lost loved ones. I can not prove this, it is just a theory of mine.

2. Prayer is important to God.

Revelation 5:8 *And when he had taken the book, the four beasts and four and twenty elders fell down before the Lamb, having every one of them harps, and golden vials full of odours, which are the prayers of saints.*

So important are our prayers, God keeps them in vials, or bottles, for remembrance.

3. Singing is an important part of worship and praise.

Revelation 5:9 *And they sung a new song, saying, Thou art worthy to take the book, and to open the seals thereof: for thou wast slain, and hast redeemed us to God by thy blood out of every kindred, and tongue, and people, and nation;*

We ought to sing more often, and we ought to teach our children to sing. The Psalms were the hymn book for the Israelites. *"Make a joyful noise unto the Lord."* Singing opens our spirit to the filling of God's Spirit. (Ephesians 5:19) I am afraid that the evil of Satan's music has crept into our homes and churches today and has opened our spirits to satanic influences.

4. Since this world is not our home, we ought to lay up treasure in Heaven. (Matthew 6:33)

It is not our job to try to save the world, but to get people out of the world. Only the Kinsman Redeemer can restore the earth.

PERSONAL APPLICATION:
1. Is there someone weeping over me in Heaven?
2. The best thing I can do for a loved one who has died is live for the Lord.
3. Have I any prayers in that bottle in Heaven?
4. Do I know and sing good godly songs? (Ephesians 5:19)
5. Am I laying up treasure down here that will be of no value five seconds after the rapture? (Matthew 6:33)

CLOSING:
This old world is sin-cursed. What a joy to know that one day soon, we are going to be "*caught up*" as John was, and we shall spend eternity with the Lord.

Looking for that blessed hope, and the glorious appearing of the great God and our Saviour Jesus Christ; (Titus 2:13)

A SEVEN-THOUSAND YEAR PROPHETIC VIEW
Chapter 10

In the beginning God created the heaven and the earth. And the earth was without form, and void; and darkness was upon the face of the deep. And the Spirit of God moved upon the face of the waters. And God said, Let there be light: and there was light. And God saw the light, that it was good: and God divided the light from the darkness. And God called the light Day, and the darkness he called Night. And the evening and the morning were the first day. (Genesis 1:1-5)

God created everything from nothing in six days. God rested on the seventh day. I believe that these seven days of creation in Genesis 1 are prophetic of 7000 years of human history on the earth. I believe each of the days of creation represent a thousand years. I believe 6000 years will pass and God will rest, and the Millennium will be ushered in. We are very close to the end of that 6000th year. I believe the rapture takes place and Daniel's 70th week is fulfilled between the sixth and the seventh prophetic days of Genesis Chapter 1. Look at the following passage as it relates to the subject at hand and pay close attention to verse eight:

2 Peter 3:1-18 This second epistle, beloved, I now write unto you; in both which I stir up your pure minds by way of remembrance:
2 That ye may be mindful of the words which were spoken before by the holy prophets, and of the commandment of us the apostles of the Lord and Saviour:
3 Knowing this first, that there shall come in the last days

scoffers, walking after their own lusts,

4 And saying, Where is the promise of his coming? for since the fathers fell asleep, all things continue as they were from the beginning of the creation.

5 For this they willingly are ignorant of, that by the word of God the heavens were of old, and the earth standing out of the water and in the water:

6 Whereby the world that then was, being overflowed with water, perished:

7 But the heavens and the earth, which are now, by the same word are kept in store, reserved unto fire against the day of judgment and perdition of ungodly men.

8 But, beloved, be not ignorant of this one thing, _that one day is with the Lord as a thousand years, and a thousand years as one day._

9 The Lord is not slack concerning his promise, as some men count slackness; but is longsuffering to us-ward, not willing that any should perish, but that all should come to repentance.

10 But the day of the Lord will come as a thief in the night; in the which the heavens shall pass away with a great noise, and the elements shall melt with fervent heat, the earth also and the works that are therein shall be burned up.

11 Seeing then that all these things shall be dissolved, what manner of persons ought ye to be in all holy conversation and godliness,

12 Looking for and hasting unto the coming of the day of God, wherein the heavens being on fire shall be dissolved, and the elements shall melt with fervent heat?

13 Nevertheless we, according to his promise, look for new heavens and a new earth, wherein dwelleth righteousness.

14 Wherefore, beloved, seeing that ye look for such things, be diligent that ye may be found of him in peace, without spot, and blameless.

*15 And account that the longsuffering of our Lord is
salvation; even as our beloved brother Paul also according
to the wisdom given unto him hath written unto you;
16 As also in all his epistles, speaking in them of these
things; in which are some things hard to be understood,
which they that are unlearned and unstable wrest, as they do
also the other scriptures, unto their own destruction.
17 Ye therefore, beloved, seeing ye know these things
before, beware lest ye also, being led away with the error of
the wicked, fall from your own stedfastness.
18 But grow in grace, and in the knowledge of our Lord and
Saviour Jesus Christ. To him be glory both now and for ever.
Amen.*

I listed this whole passage to show you some important
prophetic truths it teaches. **The whole of 2 Peter Chapter 3
is prophetic in nature**. Yes, even verse 9 and verse 18. I
underlined verse 8 because it is scorned by most preachers as
not having anything to do with prophecy. With your King
James Bible open and your thinking cap on, let us have a
little study of this passage shall we?

First, according to 2 Peter 1:1 we see that the book was
written to saved people, as is the whole Bible. *Simon Peter,
a servant and an apostle of Jesus Christ, to them that have
obtained like precious faith with us through the
righteousness of God and our Saviour Jesus Christ:*

In Chapter 3, verse 1, Peter wants to stir us up by
getting us to remember what was spoken by the prophets as
well as by the apostles of the Lord Jesus as we see in verse
2. In verse 3, Peter says there shall come scoffers in the last
days who walk after their own desires and lust. I wrote
"preachers" next to that in my Bible because your average
preacher today does not believe Christ is coming soon, nor
does he preach on prophecy. In fact most preachers hope
Christ does not come soon because it will interfere with their

church program! *Where is the promise of his coming? For since the fathers fell asleep all things continue as they were...* these scoffers say in verse four!

After all, the great men of the past believed Christ would come in their lifetime, others have set dates and were wrong, therefore why believe it anymore? In verse 5 Peter says they are *"willingly ignorant!"* In other words, men choose to be ignorant of these prophetic truths. It is one thing to be ignorant, it is quite another to be "*willingly ignorant.*" I am afraid some who read this book will choose to stay ignorant. Now notice in verses 5-7 he is speaking about the creative week of Genesis 1! Do you see it? Then in verse 8 he says, *But, beloved, be not ignorant of this one thing, that one day is with the Lord as a thousand years, and a thousand years as one day.*

What I want you to see is that right in the very middle of a prophetic chapter, and right at the end of a passage about the creative week of Genesis 1, verse 8 is stuck in there! (Verses 10-13 go on to speak of the end of this world.) *But, beloved, be not ignorant of this one thing, that <u>one day is with the Lord as a thousand years, and a thousand years as one day</u>. (2 Peter 3:8)*

Now I want to ask you, what else can verse 8 possibly mean in light of the laws of context and proper Bible interpretation? It is as plain as day to me that it is telling us **those seven days of creation are not only literal, but also prophetic of 1000 year periods of time**. What else could it possibly mean? Verse 9 shows the heart of God towards the souls of men in that He does not want people to die and go to hell in light of the fact that the end is coming soon. Verses 10-13 show that He is coming as a thief and that there will be a new earth one day and that we are to be *"looking for and hasting unto the coming of the day of God."* Verse 14 shows that we are to be striving to be found clean and holy when He comes for us. Verse 15 shows that Peter and Paul both preached this same truth. Verse 18 tells us to grow in grace because of what was said from verses 1-17. The whole chapter is prophetic in nature.

There have been many throughout history who believed this and some have even written about it. Let me give you a few quotes from some men of old concerning a 7000 year earth.

Quotes from the past

Irenaeus wrote in 150 A.D. in his book "Against Heresies" "For the day of the Lord is as a thousand years; and in six days created things were completed; **it is evident, therefore, that they will come to an end in the sixth thousand years.**"

Lactantius in 300 A.D. Wrote this in his book *Divine Institutions:* "Because all the works of God were finished in six days, **it is necessary that the world should remain in this state six ages, that is six thousand years.** Because having finished the works, He rested on the seventh day and blessed it; it is necessary that at the end of the sixth thousandth year all wickedness should be abolished out of the earth and justice should reign for a thousand years."

Bishop Latimer wrote in A.D. 1552 "**The world was ordained to endure, as all learned men affirm, 6000 years.** Now of that number, there are passed 5,552 years [as of 1,552], so there is no more left but 448 years." (Till the year 2000)

Not only did men of old believe in a 6000-year earth and then the Millennium, but look at the following Scriptures:

Come, and let us return unto the LORD: for he hath torn,

and he will heal us; he hath smitten, and he will bind us up.
After two days will he revive us: in the third day he will raise
us up, and we shall live in his sight. Hosea 6:1-2

This is a passage that is dealing specifically with the
nation of Israel. "After two days" is prophetic of the two
thousand years of the New Testament. The third day is the
one thousand year Millennial reign of Christ where Israel
will once again be the center of things on earth. My skeptical
friend, what else could it mean? Do you really think these
verses are speaking of an event that happens in three literal
days? Wait, there are more verses:

Psalm 90:4
For a thousand years in thy sight are but as yesterday when
it is past, and as a watch in the night.
Psalms 90:12
So teach us to number our days, that we may apply our
hearts unto wisdom.

Did you know that Moses wrote this Psalm and that he
will be one of the two witnesses during The Tribulation?
Does that add an interesting light on the context of the
passage?

Transfiguration teaches a 7000 year Prophetic View
And after six days Jesus taketh Peter, James, and John his
brother, and bringeth them up into an high mountain apart,
And was transfigured before them: and his face did shine as
the sun, and his raiment was white as the light. And, behold,
there appeared unto them Moses and Elias talking with him.
Then answered Peter, and said unto Jesus, Lord, it is good
for us to be here: if thou wilt, let us make here three
tabernacles; one for thee, and one for Moses, and one for
Elias. While he yet spake, behold, a bright cloud
overshadowed them: and behold a voice out of the cloud,
which said, This is my beloved Son, in whom I am well
pleased; hear ye him. Matthew 17:1-9

Here we have the story of the transfiguration. Again, all Scripture has three interpretations: the literal, the figurative, and the prophetic. This is a literal event that happened, but it also has figurative lessons to apply to our lives as well as a prophetic teaching. Verse 1 says *"after six days..."* Hey, there we have Christ appearing after six prophetic days... which are 6000 years according to II Peter 3:8. In the prophetic light of this passage, we see Jesus coming in the clouds and showing His glory to the three disciples, a type of the rapture. If you are still not convinced, look at the verse just before the chapter:

Verily I say unto you, There be some standing here, which shall not taste of death, till they see the Son of man coming in his kingdom. Matthew 16:28

The Bible goes from this verse to Matthew 17:1. What He is saying is that some will not face death, but will be raptured out of here! The *"after six days"* in verse 1 is prophetic of 6000 years of history. If that still does not convince you, in Matthew 17:3 Elijah and Moses show up after the 6000 years, and after Christ shows us His glory at the rapture. Hey, they are the two witnesses who show up in Jerusalem after the rapture and are responsible for the conversion of the 144,000 Jews at the middle of the Tribulation. When we go up in the rapture, Moses and Elijah come down to Israel. They will preach and testify to the Jews for 3 ½ years. They will be hated of all men. They will be the only light on the earth. They will be killed by the Antichrist right at the middle of the Tribulation and their bodies left in the streets for all to see. All the talk radio hosts and TV news channels will be talking about them. The whole world rejoices that they are dead. After 3 ½ days the Bible says they come back to life and ascend to Heaven exactly as Jesus did. I believe it is at this time that the 144,000 Jewish men get saved. They are all assembled there because it is the Passover Feast. They witness this event taking place probably three days later on Feast of Firstfruits which is the exact day Christ rose from the dead. Is this amazing or what? Now, why the transfiguration and why did Moses and Elijah have to meet with Jesus? Here is what I believe. <u>I believe Moses and Elijah had to see Jesus Christ in His glorified body because they are coming back to testify and be witnesses of the Messiah</u>. You have to have seen something if you are a witness, don't you? I also believe it is possible that they are the two men in white apparel at the tomb after the resurrection and the two men at the Ascension. (Luke 24:4 and Acts 1:10) Are you aware that **the only three people in the Bible that fasted for forty days are Jesus, Moses, and Elijah and they are all together at the transfiguration?** The Bible is truly a wonderful book!

***See the chapter on God's two witnesses for more on these two men I mentioned above.

In this chapter, I have tried to show you the prophetic truth of 2 Peter Chapter 3. I have showed you that the whole chapter is prophetic in nature with verse 8 stuck right in the middle. I gave some quotes from some men who lived hundreds of years ago who believed in a 6000-year earth and Sabbath rest for 1000 years. We compared Scripture with Scripture that shed more light on this thousand year earth. My friend, God punished Israel severely for not remembering and honoring the Sabbath. Would He hold them to a higher standard than He would Himself? Remember, God set the precedent for the Sabbath way back in Genesis 1. God kept the Sabbath when nobody was even looking! God rested on the seventh day! Do you think there is any chance He is going to miss His Sabbath rest after 6000 years of history? Not on your life! God IS going to have His rest after 6000 years! Check out *Hebrews 4:4 For he spake in a certain place of the seventh day on this wise, And God did rest the seventh day from all his works.*

The Old Testament ended at Calvary when the veil was rent in two. It is very possible that Calvary was 3,993 years since Adam and the seven-year tribulation is the final 7 years of the Old Testament yet to be fulfilled after the rapture. I have certainly given you some exciting things to chew on.

The following was written by my good friend Pastor Bill Waugh. We have shared a lot of prophecy together over the years. This goes along with the Genesis account of the creation story in Genesis 1 that you have just read in this chapter. Pastor Waugh does a great job of illustrating the seven days of the creative week. Whenever we would preach Prophecy Conferences together I would always encourage him to share this lesson with the folks. I believe it will be a help to you here at the end of this chapter.

THE CREATIVE WEEK
By Pastor Bill Waugh

(Genesis 1:1-5) In the beginning God created the heaven and the earth. And the earth was without form, and void; and darkness was upon the face of the deep. And the Spirit of God moved upon the face of the waters. And God said, Let there be light: and there was light. And God saw the light, that it was good: and God divided the light from the darkness. And God called the light Day, and the darkness he called Night. And the evening and the morning were the first day.
(Genesis 2:1-3) Thus the heavens and the earth were finished, and all the host of them. And on the seventh day God ended his work which he had made; and he rested on

111

the seventh day from all his work which he had made. And God blessed the seventh day, and sanctified it: because that in it he had rested from all his work which God created and made.

Let us look at the seven days of the creative week back in Genesis 1 and see how they relate to each of the 1000 year periods of history.

DAY 1 4000 B.C. — 3000 B.C.

On the first day of creation (check Ussher's date 4004 B.C. in a Scofield Bible) God divided the light from the darkness. It was at the beginning of the first 1000 years of human history that Adam and Eve chose between good and evil and fell from favor with God.

DAY 2 3000 B.C. — 2000 B.C.

It was on the second creative day that God divided the waters of the firmament. The first firmament (Pre-Flood) divided the Earth's atmosphere with what we know as space or outer space. The second firmament still forms the barrier between outer space and the Father's House (the third heaven). Can you think of anything that happened during the second 1000 years of human history that had anything to do with water? How about the Flood of Noah's day where the firmament was broken up and the fountains of the deep were opened up?

DAY 3 2000 B.C. — 1000 B.C.

On the evening and the morning of the third day, God created the grass and herbs and the fruit trees upon the dry ground. It was at the beginning of the third day of human history (check Ussher's date 2002 B.C. in a Scofield Bible) when God made a covenant with Abraham whereby the nation of Israel was formed. Most preachers agree that the fig tree mentioned throughout the New Testament is a type of Israel.

DAY 4 1000 B.C. — CHRIST

On the fourth day of creation, God created the sun the moon and the stars, which light the earth. The fourth 1000-year day of human history begins with King David sitting on the throne in Israel and ends with King Jesus the Light of the World. It is also curious to note that most of the Old Testament was written during the last thousand years of the Old Testament Age.

DAY 5 CHRIST — 1000 A.D.

It was on the fifth creative day that God created the fish to fill the waters in the seas. Christ commanded His disciples to follow Him and become fishers of men. For years, the symbol of a born-again Christian is none other than the fish.

DAY 6 1000 A.D. — PRESENT

On the sixth day of creation, God creates man; male and female and commands them to replenish the earth and subdue it. During the last one thousand years while under the curse, mankind has explored, conquered, established and divided empires. We have explored the earth, the sea, the air, and are currently exploring outer space (God's back yard).

Over the last century, we had numerous conflicts, two world wars and are currently working on a third. Today we are but a mere button-push away from complete annihilation. The book of Daniel has been unsealed. Men are running to and fro and knowledge has been increased. The earth's 1000 year Sabbath is right around the corner, and rest assured, God will remember His Sabbath and keep it holy.

DAY 7 -- THE MILLENIAL REIGN OF KING JESUS
Genesis 2:1-2
Thus the heavens and the earth were finished, and all the host of them. And on the seventh day God ended his work which he had made; and he rested on the seventh day from

all his work which he had made.

After six 1000-year days, this old sin-cursed earth will finally come to rest with King Jesus sitting on the throne of David ruling and reigning with a rod of iron and the lion shall lie down by the lamb. Praise God!

But, beloved, be not ignorant of this one thing, that one day is with the Lord as a thousand years, and a thousand years as one day.
(2 Peter 3:8)

GOD'S TWO WITNESSES
Chapter 11

(Revelation 11:3-4) And I will give power unto <u>my two</u> <u>witnesses</u>, and they shall prophesy a thousand two hundred and threescore days, clothed in sackcloth. These are the <u>two</u> <u>olive trees</u>, and the <u>two candlesticks</u> standing before the God of the earth.

The two witnesses show up after the rapture and die at the middle of the Tribulation. We saw this in an earlier chapter dealing with the transfiguration in Matthew 17. As the saints go up, God's two witnesses come down and will be witnesses in Jerusalem for 1,260 days, or 3 ½ years. They are called witnesses, candlesticks, and olive trees. They are mentioned by name in Matthew 17:1-8 and there is also a reference to them in Zechariah 4:3-12.

Why two witnesses? Why not one? I think this Scripture answers that question. *(Deuteronomy 19:15) One witness shall not rise up against a man for any iniquity, or for any sin, in any sin that he sinneth: at the mouth of two witnesses, or at the mouth of three witnesses, shall the matter be established.*

Their purpose is to proclaim the truth to Israel after the Church Age ends. All the believers are taken off the earth along with the Holy Spirit that indwells them. <u>These two</u> <u>candlesticks will be the only light left on the earth</u>. They will be hated by everyone and will be killed by the Antichrist at the middle of the Tribulation. I believe Antichrist kills them on Passover before he enters the temple and declares he is God. The two witnesses are left dead in the streets for all to see. The whole world rejoices that they are dead. There is not one saved person in the entire first half of the

Tribulation. After 3 ½ days the two witnesses are resurrected back to Heaven on Feast of Firstfruits. This is the same day Christ rose from the dead some 2000 years earlier. I believe this is when the 144,000 Jews assembled in Jerusalem for Passover trust in the Messiah. They do so after witnessing this amazing event and believe in Christ as their Messiah. Antichrist becomes furious and breaks the seven-year peace treaty and declares war on the Jews who must run for their lives. Many believe they go to Petra. This is the time period the Bible calls the "*time of Jacob's trouble.*" This is the Great Tribulation. The mark of the Beast begins here. The 144,000 Jews are the first people saved during the Tribulation. They are the "*firstfruits unto God.*" If you understand the harvest, you understand that it is in three stages. The first fruits, the main harvest, and the gleanings. The first fruits are the first crop of the garden. The main harvest is when the majority of the crop is ready. The gleanings are the corners of the field and parts that were missed in the main harvest. They are gathered later and are often left for the poor and the widows. The 144,000 are called the first fruits.

These are they which were not defiled with women; for they are virgins. These are they which follow the Lamb whithersoever he goeth. These were redeemed from among men, being the firstfruits unto God and to the Lamb. (Revelation 14:4)

Since they are the first fruits of the harvest during the Tribulation and are not saved until the middle of the Tribulation, then **there are no converts during the entire first half of the Tribulation.** This is a very sobering truth because fifty percent of the world's population die in the first half of the Tribulation, that could be as many as 3 billion people! These all go to hell. Let that sink in for a moment! Friend, some of those lost souls will be your neighbors, your friends, or co-workers. Some will lose a sister or a brother to this awful fate, some a mom or a dad. How tragic to think about! Dear friend, have you won your loved ones to Jesus Christ?

WHO CAN BE SAVED AND WHEN

It is a terrible thought to consider no souls saved in the first half of the Tribulation. I also understand that it is not a popular belief among prophecy teachers. Let me give you some Scriptures and lessons concerning why I believe nobody gets saved until the second half, and that Christ rejecters will get no second chance during the Tribulation.

1. God does have a dead-line that can be crossed.

II Thessalonians 2:1-12 and note especially verses 11&12.

And for this cause God shall send them strong delusion, that they should believe a lie: That they all might be damned who believed not the truth, but had pleasure in unrighteousness. (2 Thessalonians 2:11-12)

Many shall be purified, and made white, and tried; but the wicked shall do wickedly: and none of the wicked shall understand; but the wise shall understand. (Daniel 12:10)

Compare this with Proverbs 1:24-33. There comes a time when God shuts the door, as He did in the days of Noah.

2. All believers are gone at the rapture.

The Holy Spirit's convicting power is gone with us. There will be nobody to preach the gospel to the people left. Consider the consequences of this: *How then shall they call on him in whom they have not believed? and how shall they believe in him of whom they have not heard? and how shall they hear without a preacher? And how shall they preach, except they be sent? as it is written, How beautiful are the feet of them that preach the gospel of peace, and bring glad tidings of good things! But they have not all obeyed the gospel. For Esaias saith, Lord, who hath believed our*

117

report? So then faith cometh by hearing, and hearing by the word of God. (Romans 10:14-17)

But as we were allowed of God to be <u>put in trust with the gospel</u>, even so we speak; not as pleasing men, but God, which trieth our hearts. (1 Thessalonians 2:4)

When you study Acts 8:29-40 and Acts 10:1-48 you see that God uses Spirit-filled men to lead the lost to Jesus Christ. See also John 6:44, John 14:26 and John 16:8,13 for reference to Holy Spirit conviction being necessary to draw men to Christ. This "conviction" will not be here after the rapture.

3. Consider the open rejection by people during the Tribulation who refuse to trust Christ.

Revelation 6:15-17 and Revelation 9:17-21. Consider II Thessalonians 2:11-12 in light of this. (Quoted above)

It is because the convicting power of the Holy Spirit is gone. They can NOT be saved because the Spirit is not here to convict them of their need. Have you ever stopped to realize how important your testimony is to those around you? People need to see Christ in us. The closer we get to the end of things the less light people see in us.

4. In Revelation 14:1-4 we see that the 144,000 Jews are the first ones to be saved during the Tribulation.

They are called the "firstfruits" according to Revelation 11:13 and this takes place right at the middle, as the second woe ends in verse 14. Remember, the second woe is the fifth trumpet. *And the same hour was there a great earthquake, and the tenth part of the city fell, and in the earthquake were slain of men seven thousand: and <u>the remnant were affrighted, and gave glory to the God of heaven</u>. The second <u>woe is past</u>; and, behold, the third woe cometh quickly. (Revelation 11:13-14)*

5. Everyone on the earth rejoices at the death of God's two witnesses who are killed at the middle of the Tribulation in Revelation 11:1-13.

Verse 10 makes it clear that ALL on the earth rejoice at the news of their death. *And <u>they that dwell upon the earth shall rejoice over them</u>, and make merry, and shall send gifts one to another; because these two prophets tormented them that dwelt on the earth. (Revelation 11:10)*

6. Revelation 13:1-8 is clearly speaking of the middle of the Tribulation.

Compare Revelation 12:6-13 which speaks of Satan losing access to Heaven at the middle of the Tribulation which is what we see in Revelation 9. The "Saints" mentioned in Revelation 13:7 are the 144,000 and the people they have won to Christ.

7. Revelation 6:9-11a are the church age saints, while Revelation 6:11b are the Tribulation martyrs.

9 And when he had opened the fifth seal, I saw under the altar the souls of them that were slain for the word of God, and for the testimony which they held:

10 And they cried with a loud voice, saying, How long, O Lord, holy and true, dost thou not judge and avenge our blood on them that dwell on the earth?

11 And white robes were given unto every one of them; and it was said unto them, that they should rest yet for a little season, until their fellowservants also and their brethren, that should be killed as they were, should be fulfilled.

Almost everyone gets this wrong. <u>The souls slain for the word of God are church age saints, not Tribulation martyrs</u>. There are no saints to get martyred in the first half of the Tribulation. Look at verse 10 above. They are asking how much longer they have to wait before their blood is avenged. Friend, does that sound like someone that was just martyred a few days or weeks ago? In verse 11 they are given white robes and told to await their fellow servants that shall be killed and soon will join them. He is speaking there of the Tribulation saints who will be martyrs later. We see in Revelation 7:13-14 that they are the 144,000 Jews and their converts. *And one of the elders answered, saying unto me, What are these which are arrayed in white robes? and whence came they? And I said unto him, Sir, thou knowest. And he said to me, <u>These are they which came out of great tribulation,</u> and have washed their robes, and made them white in the blood of the Lamb. (Revelation 7:13-14)*

I see nothing in the entire Bible that shows anyone getting saved before the middle of the Tribulation. I believe many people have a false assurance that their lost loved one will get saved after the rapture. Some have even quit witnessing to them for fear of offending them and hoping they will trust the Lord after the rapture. I believe this to be a false hope.

***I have written a 73 page study guide on the book of Revelation. Many have said it has helped them in their understanding of this prophetic book. You can purchase it from my website. www.heavenboundone.net

The following is from my Revelation Study Guide concerning Chapter 11 and the two witnesses. If there is some repetition here, you will understand why.

(Revelation 11:1-14) And there was given me a reed like unto a rod: and the angel stood, saying, Rise, and measure the temple of God, and the altar, and them that worship therein. But the court which is without the temple leave out, and measure it not; for it is given unto the Gentiles: and the holy city shall they tread under foot forty and two months. And I will give power unto my two witnesses, and they shall prophesy a thousand two hundred and threescore days, clothed in sackcloth. These are the two olive trees, and the two candlesticks standing before the God of the earth. And if any man will hurt them, fire proceedeth out of their mouth, and devoureth their enemies: and if any man will hurt them, he

120

must in this manner be killed. These have power to shut heaven, that it rain not in the days of their prophecy: and have power over waters to turn them to blood, and to smite the earth with all plagues, as often as they will. And when they shall have finished their testimony, the beast that ascendeth out of the bottomless pit shall make war against them, and shall overcome them, and kill them. And their dead bodies shall lie in the street of the great city, which spiritually is called Sodom and Egypt, where also our Lord was crucified. And they of the people and kindreds and tongues and nations shall see their dead bodies three days and an half, and shall not suffer their dead bodies to be put in graves. And they that dwell upon the earth shall rejoice over them, and make merry, and shall send gifts one to another; because these two prophets tormented them that dwelt on the earth. And after three days and an half the Spirit of life from God entered into them, and they stood upon their feet; and great fear fell upon them which saw them. And they heard a great voice from heaven saying unto them, Come up hither. And they ascended up to heaven in a cloud; and their enemies beheld them. And the same hour was there a great earthquake, and the tenth part of the city fell, and in the earthquake were slain of men seven thousand: and the remnant were affrighted, and gave glory to the God of heaven. The second woe is past; and, behold, the third woe cometh quickly.

Revelation Chapter 11 is a parenthetical chapter. It is inserted to explain some things. If you do not understand what a parenthetical chapter is, you will never get the timeline for Revelation. A parenthetical chapter is a parenthesis. It is something stuck in to add some information but is not in order. You could skip over a parenthesis and not lose the context. Often, as is the case here, a parenthetical passage will go back in time and give more details about an event. This is why so many get the Tribulation Period out of order. The Revelation is in order but you have to understand there are these "parentheses" stuck in to help explain in more detail.

Let's look at this chapter that is misunderstood by so many. The chapter takes us back to the beginning of the Tribulation to explain something important that has been going on. Verses 1 and 2 are letting us know that the

121

attention after the rapture is on the Jews, not the church. Daniel 9:24 makes it clear that the Tribulation is not about the church. The church is in Heaven, for there are no Christians left after Revelation 4:1. The measuring of the temple lets us know that after the rapture, the Jews will begin their Old Testament temple sacrifices again. The rod symbolizes the judgment to come upon them. The temple will either be rebuilt just prior to or right after the rapture. It is very possible that Antichrist will build it for them as part of the peace treaty. It is to be built on the very spot where the Muslim Dome of the Rock is now. You have surely seen pictures of this or seen it in the news. It is a big gold-colored, dome-shaped building. I actually went inside it in 1979. It sits on holy ground, the very spot on which the new temple will be built. I look for something to happen to the Dome soon. This revival of Old Testament temple worship is not a good thing, for it pictures a coming Messiah rather than a crucified and risen Messiah. Revelation 11:2 lets us know that though Israel has the temple sacrifices going again, the Gentiles are all around them. The Antichrist is going to make a peace treaty with Israel right after the rapture. They will be at peace while the whole world is at war. Kind of backwards from how it has been, is it not? *And after threescore and two weeks shall <u>Messiah be cut off</u>, but not for himself: and the people of the prince that shall come shall destroy the city and the sanctuary; and the end thereof shall be with a flood, and unto the end of the war desolations are determined. And he shall confirm the covenant with many for one week: and in the midst of the week he shall cause the sacrifice and the oblation to cease, and for the overspreading of abominations he shall make it desolate, even until the consummation, and that determined shall be poured upon the desolate. Daniel 9:26-27*

Do you see how important the book of Daniel is to the

understanding of Revelation, especially Daniel chapter 9? *"Messiah cut off"* speaks of Calvary, the *"prince that shall come"* is the Antichrist, the same person that is referred to in verse 27. He, the Antichrist, will confirm the covenant, make a treaty with Israel for one week, which is seven years. Right in the middle of the week of seven years, he puts an end to the temple sacrifices, goes into the temple himself and declares he is God, (Matthew 24:15-21) and demands Israel worship him. This proves that Israel is going to resume the temple worship during the first half of the Tribulation. I believe that all this happens just as Satan loses his access to Heaven (Revelation 12) and then the devils from the pit are loosed here on earth. (Revelation 9) This is the moment the Jews realize the truth about Jesus being the Messiah and 144,000 get saved. This all ushers in the second half of the Tribulation, called in Matthew 24:21 *"The Great Tribulation."* It is referred to as *"the time of Jacob's trouble"* because it is Satan warring against the Jews. (Revelation 12:12-13)

Now, Revelation 11:3-14 deals with the theme of this chapter, the two witnesses. They are called Olive trees, and candlesticks. They show up right after the rapture, and they are the only light on the earth for the first half of the Tribulation. I realize that many people say they show up during the second half, but I disagree. I will show you why shortly. The Bible does not say who these two witnesses are in this passage, but it is certain that they are men and not angels. Most people believe they are either Enoch and Elijah, or Moses and Elijah. Whoever they are, they are filled with the power of God and are able to do great miracles. <u>It is my belief from the transfiguration given in Matthew 17 that these men are Moses and Elijah.</u> In Revelation 11:7, the beast kills them and leaves their bodies in the streets of Jerusalem, but not until they have finished

123

their work for God. Verse 10 gives us some proof that nobody is yet saved on the earth, as it says "*they that dwell upon the earth shall rejoice over them and make merry*" over the death of these two prophets of God. That certainly gives the impression that everyone on earth is glad that these prophets are dead. (That means nobody is saved yet, unless you think there are Christians on the moon.) In verse 11, the two candlesticks are brought back to life before the eyes of the whole world and ascend to Heaven. In verse 13, I believe the 144,000 get saved as a direct result of the testimony of these two witnesses. I believe the reason why the 144,000 are in Jerusalem is because it is Passover week. I believe the Antichrist kills Elijah and Moses on Passover, enters the temple and declares he is God. 3 ½ days later would be Feast of Firstfruits, the day Jesus rose from the grave. I believe this is the day the two witnesses ascend to Heaven. Now, look closely at Revelation 11:14 *The second woe is past; and, behold, the third woe cometh quickly.* Did you see what that said? This is more proof that the chapter is parenthetical, and that these things we just read about from verses 1-13 are the first half of the Tribulation. This also proves the arrival of the two witnesses are in the first half. Do you see it? It said the second woe is past. Remember, the second woe is the sixth trumpet that sounded during the beginning of the second half of the Tribulation period in Revelation 9:13. So you see, these two witnesses show up in the first half of the Tribulation not the second half as many Bible teachers say. This chapter has been explaining some things about the first half of the Tribulation in verses 1-14 which we know have already happened back in Chapter 9, proving it is a review, a parenthetical chapter. Even parenthetical chapters have a sequence of order as is seen in the very next verses. Revelation 11:15-19 speaks of the seventh trumpet which is the third woe. So the first fourteen verses explain the first half, and a bit past the middle, while verses 15-19 continue with the second half of the Tribulation. The seventh trumpet of verse 15 is actually explained in Revelation 15:1 with the seven vials.

The chronological timeline of the Tribulation is as follows: Revelation Chapter 6, Chapter 8, Chapter 9, Chapter 11:15-19, Chapter 15, Chapter 16, Chapter 19:1-11. The other chapters are important, but not in chronological order. They are added to explain some things. They are parenthetical.

LESSONS:

1. The Tribulation is going to happen just as God planned.

2. God always leaves some light. These two prophets will be the only light left on the earth after the rapture for 3 1/2 years. The church is gone, all believers are gone, and the restraining power of the Holy Spirit over evil has been lifted. (2 Thessalonians 2:1-4)

3. The Devil is no match for Spirit-filled Christians. The beast has no power over the two prophets until God lets him.

4. The world rejoices when Christians fall.

PERSONAL APPLICATION:

1. Am I in the plan and will of God? (Romans 12:1-2)

2. Do I bring the light of Jesus to my small part of the world? (Matthew 5:16)

3. Am I filled with the Holy Spirit of God right now? (Ephesians 5:18)

4. When you fall, shock the world by getting back up. (Proverbs 24:16)

CLOSING: Compare Revelation 11:18 with Daniel 9:2 and see how they go together in showing the purpose of the Tribulation.

*So likewise ye,
when ye shall see
all these things,
know that it is near,
even at the doors.*
(Matthew 24:33)

SIGNS FOR THE LAST DAYS
Chapter 12

He answered and said unto them, When it is evening, ye say, It will be fair weather: for the sky is red. And in the morning, It will be foul weather to day: for the sky is red and lowring. O ye hypocrites, ye can discern the face of the sky; but can ye not discern the signs of the times? (Matthew 16:2-3)

Are we living in the last days? Let me start out by saying that the Bible teaches that we have been in the last days since Christ rose from the dead. Look at what the Scripture says: *Hebrews 1:2 Hath in **these last days** spoken unto us by his Son, whom he hath appointed heir of all things, by whom also he made the worlds;* See, since Jesus came, God says we have been in "the last days". Look at *Acts 2:17: And it shall come to pass **in the last days**, saith God, I will pour out of my Spirit upon all flesh: and your sons and your daughters shall prophesy, and your young men shall see visions, and your old men shall dream dreams:* This actually was prophesied in Joel 2:28-32 and most of this was fulfilled in Acts 2 on the day of Pentecost, as Peter points out for us here.

Notice that this Scripture along with Joel 2 is speaking of the last days which started during the New Testament Age. Nevertheless, the Bible also speaks of the last days in another sense. I believe that God speaks of the drawing nigh of the second coming of Christ, which is preceded by the rapture and the seven-year Tribulation, as the last days. I call it The Last of the Last days. Look with me at what the Bible says in *2 Peter 3:3-4: Knowing this first, that there shall come in the last days scoffers, walking after their own lusts, And saying, Where is the promise of his coming? for since the fathers fell asleep, all things continue as they were from the beginning of the creation.*

Did you notice that while Peter is writing some years AFTER the resurrection, he speaks of some terrible events that SHALL COME in the last days? Obviously, he is speaking of the last of the last days, a future event and the time that you and I are living in right now. Let me give you another important passage that I think will shed more light on the subject:

2 Timothy 3:1-5: *This know also, that in the last days perilous times shall come. For men shall be lovers of their own selves, covetous, boasters, proud, blasphemers, disobedient to parents, unthankful, unholy, Without natural affection, trucebreakers, false accusers, incontinent, fierce, despisers of those that are good, Traitors, heady, highminded, lovers of pleasures more than lovers of God; Having a form of godliness, but denying the power thereof: from such turn away.*

Did you notice that Paul makes the same point that Peter did? Paul said that perilous times shall come, speaking of a FUTURE event. Paul, while living in the last days, the New Testament Age, says that in the future, in the last days, these signs will be prevalent. Are you with me so far? We have been in the LAST DAYS since Jesus, but the Bible speaks of the last of the last days which are the time right before the rapture. Now that I have made that clear, let me give you some reasons I strongly believe we are living in the last of the last days.

I. Because of the signs given in 2 Tim 3:1-5

Look back at the Scripture above, and notice the signs he gave of how things would be in the last days: *Lovers of their own selves,* me, my, mine. Does that sound like us?

128

Covetous, keeping up with the Jones's. Got to have what the neighbor has; *boasters, braggers, proud, blasphemers, disobedient to parents,* the streets are full of them. *Unthankful, unholy, without natural affection,* my friend, how is it that millions of babies have been aborted? How about the small amount of time that parents spend with their children today, with their work schedules, daycare, selfish divorces, etc.? *Trucebreakers,* my friend, a man's word used to mean something, but not so today. *False accusers, incontinent, fierce, despisers of those that are good, traitors, heady, highminded, lovers of pleasures more than lovers of God;* Folks, the lakes and pools and movie houses are full on Sunday while the church is nearly empty. *Having a form of godliness,* this is our religious crowd. They have the talk, but they are ungodly. My friend, the signs of the times point to the soon return of Christ.

II. Because of the increased ease and use of travel in our generation.

Daniel 12:4 *But thou, O Daniel, shut up the words, and seal the book, even to the time of the end: many shall run to and fro, and knowledge shall be increased.*

Many shall "run to and fro" is a sign given of the time of the end. It is amazing how travel has changed over the years. Did you know that for about 5,800 years of human history, man could only travel as fast as a horse could carry him? In the early 1800's the invention of the train with its steam engine changed everything. They called it the "iron horse." It revolutionized the world and was basically the start of the industrial age. From that time forward things have literally accelerated. Now things are changing so fast you can't keep up with them. As soon as a laptop or i-Phone makes it to the stores they are coming out with the next generation of gadgets.

III. The tremendous and almost frightening increase and availability of knowledge.

Daniel 12:4 But thou, O Daniel, shut up the words, and seal the book, even to the time of the end: many shall run to and fro, and knowledge shall be increased.

It is amazing when you think how fast the access of knowledge is since the computer came about. In addition, every year they are smarter, faster, and easier to use. These are signs the word of God is giving us of what it will be like in the last days before Christ returns.

IV. Lack of faith is a sign of the end.

Look what Jesus said concerning the time of His return in Luke 18:8. *I tell you that he will avenge them speedily. Nevertheless when the Son of man cometh, shall he find faith on the earth?*

The average person does not even know how to define faith, let alone live by faith. Let me give you a definition of faith from Hebrews Chapter 11. Faith is believing that God will do what He said in the Bible He will do. Apart from the truths in the Bible, a person cannot even practice faith. We see our generation trusting in Government, not God, in money not prayer, in insurance rather than Scripture. Now I am not against these things, I am just saying that we are not to put our trust in them.

V. The fact that the average born again child of God does not believe Jesus is coming soon, is possibly one of the greatest signs of all that He is coming back Soon, and we are in fact living in the last days.

Luke 12:40 Be ye therefore ready also: for the Son of man cometh at an hour when ye think not.

The Church is fast asleep! Christ's coming is drawing near, but the average Christian is eating, drinking, and being merry as they did in Noah's day. The Bible says, *"No man knoweth the day or the hour"*, but the Bible also says:

1 Thessalonians 5:1 But of the times and the seasons, brethren, ye have no need that I write unto you. 2 For yourselves know perfectly that the day of the Lord so cometh as a thief in the night. 3 For when they shall say, Peace and safety; then sudden destruction cometh upon them, as travail upon a woman with child; and they shall not escape.
4 But ye, brethren, are not in darkness, that that day should overtake you as a thief. 5 Ye are all the children of light, and the children of the day: we are not of the night, nor of darkness. 6 Therefore let us not sleep, as do others; but let us watch and be sober.

My friend, we may not know the exact day, month or year, but God has given us signs. Verse 4 tells us we are not in darkness, and the day of Christ's coming does not have to catch us off guard. Let's look for His coming, let's live holy lives, let's win everyone to Christ that we can before it is too late. He told us to *"Watch and be sober."* Let us live as if we expect He may come back for us today!

VI. Because in our generation, for the first time in history, one man can effectively rule the whole world.

Through the technology of computers, satellite, phones, and the high speed of travel, one man could actually rule the whole world. The Antichrist will rule the world after we are gone. The high tech of recent years has made it possible for one man to sit in an office just about anywhere in the world and communicate with the whole world. Already it is happening. Our President, from the comfort of the Oval Office, simply gives the word and a drone can take out a rogue leader on the other side of the ocean. Our President can pretty much communicate any message he chooses and it will be transmitted around the globe. Never before has a generation been able to rule like they can in our generation. It is easy for us to understand the mark of the beast and a system where no one can buy or sell without it. We use it every day of our lives without even thinking about it. How many understood any of this... even fifty years ago? Today, we can understand prophesy, the mark of the beast, and world destruction like no other generation of people ever has. Daniel 12:9 *And he said, Go thy way, Daniel: for the words are closed up and sealed till the time of the end.*

VII. Because of the developments in Israel in our generation.

Preachers that know Bible prophecy will tell you to "keep your eyes on Israel." You see, the end-times (Tribulation) are all about Israel, not the Church. Let me give you some facts about Israel that are signs of Christ's soon return:

1. Israel was recognized by the world as a nation in May 1948. Do you understand that no other nation in the history of the world has ever ceased to exist and then years later recovered their statehood? None except one that is, Israel. Great Britain got Israel in the Balfour Agreement in 1917. The U.N. (and Britain) gave the land of Israel to the Jews in May 1948. Israel got Jerusalem in 1967 after the miraculous Six-Day War. I lean towards 1967 as *"The fig tree buddeth."* fulfillment of Matthew 24:*32 Now learn a parable of the fig tree; When his branch is yet tender, and putteth forth leaves, ye know that summer is nigh*: What is Israel without Jerusalem?

2. The anointing oil needed to anoint the high priest, as well as Jesus, has been discovered after nearly 2000 years. The tree this oil comes from has been extinct for years. In 70 A.D. when Jerusalem was destroyed, some flasks of this oil were hidden under ground and were just discovered in recent years.

3. I have read that they now have the Red Heifer needed for the sacrifice.

4. Everything needed for rebuilding the temple is ready. Many more things could be mentioned, but understand that Israel is more ready for the events of the Tribulation than ever before in history! Read Matthew 24 and you will see that the temple must be ready right after the rapture. As was said earlier, it is possible that the Antichrist will in fact build the temple for them after they sign the seven-year peace treaty. Either way, the Temple could be up in a matter of a few short weeks.

5. Because of the dam on the Euphrates River. The Bible speaks of the Euphrates River drying up and the kings of the east crossing to invade Israel. This would be China. Right now, there is a dam already in place that can stop the river from flowing, making way for the "Kings of the East."

Revelation 16:12 And the sixth angel poured out his vial upon the great river Euphrates; and the water thereof was dried up, that the way of the kings of the east might be prepared.

VIII. Because we live in the generation that for the first time in history has the power to destroy itself.

Mark 13:20 makes it clear that at the final battle at the end of the seven years, the nations would have destroyed themselves unless Christ had come.

And except that the Lord had shortened those days, no flesh should be saved: but for the elect's sake, whom he hath chosen, he hath shortened the days.

Military people say that Russia right now has 10,000 ICBM's aimed at the United States of America. Each one of these intercontinental ballistic missiles is more powerful than the bombs dropped on Japan! From the time the button is pushed, it takes about 15 minutes to reach its target here in America. Imagine if even half of them make it through, America would cease to exist! Experts say that the ICBM's in Russia will become unusable in the near future. If they are going to use them, it will have to be soon. Many small nations around the world now have some nuclear weapons. North Korea announced that it has nukes. Iran is very close to having nukes. It would not take much for a worldwide nuclear war to break out. America is believed to have bombs that are so powerful they have not even been tested!

Notice in the first four seals of Revelation 6 that 1/4th of the world's population will die as a result of war. That is around 1 billion souls! In the first half of the Tribulation, half the world's population will die and go to an eternity in hell. Never before has a generation understood this prophecy like we can. George Washington, with his black powder musket, certainly could not understand it like we can. People in 1945 could not understand what you and I understand today. The world is more unstable than it has ever been in history. The financial markets, oil, nukes, terrorism, over crowded prisons, sodomy, greed and lust are all trademarks of the last days. You and I had better get ready for the return of the Lord!

IX. Because of the description given of the last church on earth before the trumpet sounds.

We are speaking of the Laodicean Church
Revelation 3:14-18
And unto the angel of the church of the Laodiceans write;
These things saith the Amen, the faithful and true witness,
the beginning of the creation of God; I know thy works, that
thou art neither cold nor hot: I would thou wert cold or hot.
So then because thou art lukewarm, and neither cold nor hot,
I will spue thee out of my mouth. Because thou sayest, I am
rich, and increased with goods, and have need of nothing;
and knowest not that thou art wretched, and miserable, and
poor, and blind, and naked: I counsel thee to buy of me gold
tried in the fire, that thou mayest be rich; and white raiment,
that thou mayest be clothed, and that the shame of thy

nakedness do not appear; and anoint thine eyes with eyesalve, that thou mayest see.

This is a description of the average church on earth just preceding the rapture. Does wall to wall carpeting, big screen monitors, and a look at us attitude seem too familiar? Look at the description of this church: Lukewarm, wretched, miserable, poor, blind, and naked. This is a type of the church that shall be in existence at the rapture and it clearly fits the characteristics of most churches and believers today.

Remember, all Scripture has three interpretations. The literal, the figurative, and the prophetic. These seven churches in Revelation 2 and 3 are literal churches that existed in John's day. They also have a figurative lesson for us today. However, in light of Revelation being a prophetic book, the main teaching for us is a prophetic one.

These seven churches are prophetic of seven periods of the 2000-year Church Age. The Laodicean Church is prophetic of the Age before Jesus comes back. When you turn the page to Revelation 4:1, the rapture takes place.
After this I looked, and, behold, a door was opened in heaven: and the first voice which I heard was as it were of a trumpet talking with me; which said, <u>Come up hither</u>, and I will shew thee things which must be hereafter.

There is no more mention of the church until after the Second Coming of Christ in Revelation 19:11.

X. Because the whole world seems to be groaning in want and expectation of some catastrophic event.
Romans 8:22 For we know that the whole creation groaneth and travaileth in pain together until now.
Matthew 24:3-8 And as he sat upon the mount of Olives, the disciples came unto him privately, saying, Tell us, when shall these things be? and what shall be the sign of thy coming, and of the end of the world? And Jesus answered and said unto them, Take heed that no man deceive you. For many

*shall come in my name, saying, I am Christ; and shall
deceive many. And ye shall hear of wars and rumours of
wars: see that ye be not troubled: for all these things must
come to pass, but the end is not yet. For nation shall rise
against nation, and kingdom against kingdom: and there
shall be famines, and pestilences, and earthquakes, in divers
places. All these are the beginning of sorrows.*

In the Olivet discourse in Matthew 24, the things
mentioned in verses 5-8 appear to be warning signs, or you
could say, tremors leading up to the big quake.
*Matthew 24:33 So likewise ye, when ye shall see all these
things, know that it is near, even at the doors.*
Just think of the tremendous increase in natural disasters
in just the last few years alone. Doesn't it just feel like
something is about to happen? Something big?
In closing this chapter, let me give you one more
important fact that shows we are very near the end of this
age. I believe there are going to be 7000 years of history
down here. This was discussed already, but consider the
following: God's special number is seven. It is the number
of perfection and completeness. There are seven notes in a
scale, seven colors in the rainbow. It is God's number.
There are seven churches in Revelation, seven trumpets,
seven seals. There are seven days of creation. Those seven
days are prophetic of 7000 years of history. There are seven
major feasts for Israel, and something big happened on each
of those feast days. Christ died on Feast of Passover, lay in
the grave on Feast of Unleavened Bread, He rose on Feast of
Firstfruits, and The Church was empowered on Feast of
Pentecost. These four feasts look back at what has taken
place. The first four feasts have been fulfilled perfectly right
to the day. The next three feasts look forward. The Feast of
Trumpets is a type of the rapture. Many believe Christ will

come on the Feast of Trumpets. It certainly would be the day I would choose, but I am not God. Then the Feast of Day of Atonement, Yom Kippur, a perfect time for the second coming of Christ, and followed by Feast of Tabernacles, a type of the Millennium, God's rest. The seven days of creation are a type of seven thousand years of the world.

2 Peter 3:8 But, beloved, be not ignorant of this one thing, that one day is with the Lord as a thousand years, and a thousand years as one day.

Compare that with *Hosea 6:2 After two days will he revive us: in the third day he will raise us up, and we shall live in his sight.* This is speaking of God dealing with the Jews after the 2000 year Church Age!

Psalm 90:4 For a thousand years in thy sight are but as yesterday when it is past, and as a watch in the night.

Interesting, this Psalm was written by Moses who will be one of the two witnesses during the first half of the Tribulation. These verses clearly hint at a 7000-year period of history down here on the earth! If that is true, and we need the last 1000 years for the Millennial reign, then we are just about at the end! We are right now on the verge of the 6000th year. If we are very close to the end of the 6000th year of history, don't you think God will have His Sabbath rest? Do you really think that God will put it off for a few years? He punished Israel for not remembering the Sabbath; I do not believe He will be late. Now, I realize that the year 2000 is past, but the calendar is not right. The New Testament Church Age did not start at the birth of Jesus, but at Calvary, that is some 33 ½ years later. The calendar is off; it has been messed with. Bishop Ussher put the birth of Christ at 4 B.C. That means Christ was born four years before Christ! They were trying to make it all come out right. You can not trust the calendar. God does not use the solar calendar of 365 1/4th days anywhere in Scripture. God uses the prophetic 360 day calendar. We can not be sure where we are as far as the 2000 years of the New Testament. We must be very close though.

This is no time to be backslidden! Get your heart right with the Lord today! Decide to start doing more for God than you ever have before. Live your life as if He may come today. There is too much prophecy in the Bible to ignore it. God told Daniel to *"seal up the book till the time of the end."* My friend, we are in that time of the end right now!

And he said, Behold, I will make thee know what shall be in the last end of the indignation: for at the time appointed the end shall be.

(Daniel 8:19)

PROPHETIC FIGURES AND TYPES
Chapter 13

The Bible is filled with figures and types. Many of these figures have a prophetic interpretation. Look at the following Scriptures.

Hebrews 9:24 For Christ is not entered into the holy places made with hands, which are the figures of the true; but into heaven itself, now to appear in the presence of God for us:

Hebrews 9:9 Which was a figure for the time then present, in which were offered both gifts and sacrifices, that could not make him that did the service perfect, as pertaining to the conscience;

Hebrews 8:4-5 For if he were on earth, he should not be a priest, seeing that there are priests that offer gifts according to the law: Who serve unto the example and shadow of heavenly things, as Moses was admonished of God when he was about to make the tabernacle: for, See, saith he, that thou make all things according to the pattern shewed to thee in the mount.

Colossians 2:17 Which are a shadow of things to come; but the body is of Christ.

I have already given some prophetic views of Mary and Martha as well as the Jewish wedding. We spent a great deal of time on the seven feasts and the Jubilee. We saw the wonderful prophetic truths of the transfiguration of Christ and we saw how the six days of creation are prophetic of 6000 years of history. We are going to take this chapter and look at a few more figures and types in the Bible that have a prophetic interpretation.

Joseph is Prophetic of Jesus.

There are some amazing similarities between Joseph in the book of Genesis, and the Lord Jesus Christ. The Bible is filled with figures and types. I'm not going to take a lot of time or space to list all the Scriptures. I just want to give you a rough outline. Let me just list them here for you.

1. Both Jesus and Joseph were beloved of their Father.

2. Joseph had a coat of many colors. Jesus had a coat for which the soldiers gambled.

3. Joseph was sent to seek out his brothers and bring them bread. Jesus, the "bread of life" was sent to seek and to save that which was lost.

4. Joseph was rejected and despised of his brothers. *Jesus, a man of sorrows, despised and rejected of men.* (Isaiah 53) *He came unto his own, and his own received him not.* (John 1:11)

5. Joseph was thrown into a pit; Jesus went to the lower parts of the earth.

6. Joseph was sold into slavery. Jesus was sold for 30 pieces of silver.

7. Joseph and Jesus both spent time in Egypt.

8. Joseph and Jesus were both falsely accused.

9. Joseph and Jesus both suffered unjustly.

10. Joseph was sent to prison, Jesus to the cross and the tomb.

11. Joseph survived prison and sat on the right hand of the most high Pharaoh. Jesus overcame the grave to sit at the right hand of the Most High God!

12. Joseph was given a Gentile bride. Jesus was also given a Gentile bride, the Church.

13. Joseph's brothers, the Jews, came into Egypt three times seeking bread. Remember, because of the famine, Jacob sent them to buy bread. Three times the Jews have entered the

land of promise. First in the book of Exodus, second after the 70-year captivity, and the third time in 1948/1967.

14. Joseph's brothers came face to face with him but did not recognize him. Jesus came face to face with Israel but they did not recognize Him as the Messiah. The Jews for the most part are still blinded.

15. Joseph revealed himself to his Jewish brothers after the third time they entered the land of Egypt, but ONLY after he ordered all the Gentiles out of the room. Remember, he ordered the Egyptians out, and then shocked his brothers when he said, *"I am Joseph, does my father yet live?"* Hey, Israel has entered the Promised Land three times now. Jesus is getting ready to reveal Himself to them, but ONLY after He orders all the Gentiles off the earth at the rapture. *"I am Jesus whom thou persecutest..."* Jesus said to Saul of Tarsus. It will not be long; we are going to be taken out of the way!

The Story of Esther is prophetic.

For if thou altogether holdest thy peace at this time, then shall there enlargement and deliverance arise to the Jews from another place; but thou and thy father's house shall be destroyed: and who knoweth whether thou art come to the kingdom for such a time as this? (Esther 4:14)

The name of God is not mentioned even once in the book of Esther, yet you will find Him on every page. The story of Esther takes place at the end of the 70 year Babylonian captivity somewhere around 520-530 B.C. The literal version is that King Ahasuerus invited Queen Vashti to the feast he was hosting. Her disobedience in refusing to come angered not only the king, but the dignitaries at the feast as well. They were concerned that this would set a bad precedent, and that wives throughout the kingdom would

141

begin to rebel against the will of their husbands too. It could start a women's liberation movement! It was decided that Queen Vashti would be put away from the presence of the king and was never to see his face again. All the young virgins of the land were brought to the palace and the king eventually chose Esther to be his new queen. Esther was in fact a Jew but had changed her name at the advice of her cousin Mordecai. This was done to hide her identity. It was not popular to be a Jew then, nor has it ever been. As the story goes, we see a man named Haman, the king's right hand man, who hates the Jews. A gallows is built for Mordecai to be hung on, and a date is chosen for the extermination of all the Jews. The date is Adar 13th and 14th. That is in our month of December. The king signs the decree without really understanding what it meant. When Mordecai learns of it, he gets a message to Queen Esther. He asks her to go to the king and plead for their lives. In those days you did not just walk in to see the king like we would today. Even the queen had to be called and invited to stand in the presence of the king. If you showed up without being summoned, and the king did not lift his scepter, the guards would kill you. Esther asked the Jews to fast and pray. She then went before the king who raised the golden scepter and allowed her to come before him. She asked the king to come to a banquet she would prepare and to bring Haman. At the banquet she asked the king and Haman to come again the next night to another banquet she would prepare. It was agreed. That night the king could not sleep and asked for the chronicles to be brought so he could read. He came to a place in the record where it was recorded that Mordecai had saved his life. He asked what had been done for this man and found that no reward or gesture had been made. The next day he asks Haman what should be done for one in whom the king delights. Haman, being the proud man that he was, thought the king was speaking of him and began to tell the king what he should do to honor such a man. The king then told Haman to go and do so for Mordecai the Jew, who was sitting in the courtyard in sackcloth at that very moment. You can imagine the anger that Haman had. He had a gallows built and planned to kill Mordecai that evening after the banquet. That evening after the banquet was over, Queen Esther revealed that she was a Jew and pleaded for her life and the lives of the Jews. The king is shocked and troubled. He goes out to think and while he is gone Haman comes to Esther's side and pleads for his life. At that moment the king returns and sees what appears to be Haman forcing himself on the queen. They cover his head and take him out and hang him on the very gallows Haman had built for Mordecai. What an amazing story. By the way, the date just happens to be the 17th of Nisan which is the Feast of Firstfruits. Deliverance came to the Jews this night. The law could not be undone. It was the law of the Medes and Persians, which could not be undone. What they did was give all the Jews permission to defend themselves on Adar 13th from those who would come to kill them. It was a great victory for the Jews. Mordecai was made second in the land just as Joseph was in Egypt. Adar 13th and 14th became the feast of Purim. They celebrate it even to this day. We mentioned it in the chapter called 2520. This took place approximately 2,520 years ago. Now, that is a brief summary of the story. Let me give you a brief prophetic interpretation of the story.

King Ahasuerus represents God. Queen Vashti represents the Jews, the nation of Israel. The Lord shows up and says "The Kingdom of Heaven is at hand." The Jews, represented by Vashti, refuse to come. The Lord puts away Israel and chooses a Gentile bride (the church) represented by Esther. Mordecai would represent the Hebrew Prophets and

143

Apostles. Haman represents the Antichrist who hates the Jews because they brought Messiah into the world. It is also interesting in the story that Haman has 10 sons who are all killed in Esther 9:13. The ten sons would be a type of the ten nations that Antichrist rules over. Daniel talked about the ten toes and the ten horns. Read the book of Esther and see if these things start to make sense.

THE SEVEN CHURCHES

There are seven churches mentioned in Revelation 2 and 3. They are actual churches that existed. John was told to write to each one of them. However, there is also a prophetic interpretation of these seven churches that I want you to see. Though I believe that these are literal churches that existed, **I believe they represent the entire 2000 year church age.** Let me give you some reasons I am certain of this:

1) Because the first verse of the Revelation shows that it is a prophetic book of things to come.

Revelation 1:1 The Revelation of Jesus Christ, which God gave unto him, to shew unto his servants things which must shortly come to pass; and he sent and signified it by his angel unto his servant John:

2) Because of the chronological order of the seven churches in the book. The rapture takes place in Chapter 4 right after the last of the seven churches is mentioned. That last church is a cold and dead church that the Bible says will exist at the rapture.

3) Looking back, we can clearly see all seven of these church ages in history.

4) The number of the churches, seven, signifies completion.

144

THE FIG TREE

Now learn a parable of the fig tree; When his branch is yet tender, and putteth forth leaves, ye know that summer is nigh: So likewise ye, when ye shall see all these things, know that it is near, even at the doors. Verily I say unto you, This generation shall not pass, till all these things be fulfilled. (Matthew 24:32-34)

Nearly every student of the Bible agrees that the fig tree is a type of the nation of Israel. I believe the fig tree was planted in 1948 and 'budded" in 1967 after the Six-Day War when they acquired Jerusalem.

THE HARVEST

The harvest of a crop has an obvious prophetic meaning. The rapture is a harvest of souls. The seven feasts of the Lord revolve around the harvest.

*Blessed and holy is he that hath part in the <u>first resurrection</u>: on such the second death hath no power, but they shall be priests of God and of Christ, and shall reign with him a thousand years. (*Revelation 20:6)

This is speaking of bodily resurrections. There are two resurrections. The first is for the saved, the second is for the lost. When a believer died before the cross his body went in the ground and his soul and spirit went to Abraham's bosom as seen in Luke 16:19-31. This is the place called "Paradise" that Christ promised to the thief on the cross in Luke 23:43, which is so misunderstood today. Man is a three-fold being consisting of a spirit, soul, and body. *And the very God of peace sanctify you wholly; and I pray God your whole <u>spirit and soul and body</u> be preserved blameless unto the coming of our Lord Jesus Christ. (1 Thessalonians 5:23)* Note the order in which God places them. The spirit is the part of man that can commune or fellowship with God. That is the

145

part of man that is dead when he is born and must be regenerated, quickened (made alive) at salvation. The soul is the seat of the emotions, our intellect. The body is the flesh that we can see. Man seems to always get the order backwards. Most preachers say it backwards. To us, the order of importance is the body, the soul, and then the spirit. When a believer died in the Old Testament his body went to the grave, and his soul and spirit went to paradise, Abraham's bosom. God is a Trinity: the Father, Son, and Holy Ghost. Jesus is a three-fold being too. When Jesus was dying he cried out in Luke 23:46 *"...Father, into thy hands I commend my spirit:...?* Yet, He told the thief, *"...To day shalt thou be with me in paradise." (Luke 23:43)* Then we see the body of our Saviour placed in a tomb. Now which is it? Where did the Lord go after He paid the sin debt of the world on the cross of Calvary? He went to all three. His Spirit went to the Father, His soul went to Abraham's bosom, and His body went to the grave.

***Contact me for a study on Abraham's Bosom and O.T. salvation.

When Christ paid the penalty for sin, He became the first to rise bodily from the dead. He lead the O.T. saints in Paradise to Heaven. Since the cross, the spirit and soul of all believers who die go to Heaven to be with the Lord. (Ephesians 4:8-10) However, we do not have our resurrected glorified bodies yet. At the rapture, all the bodies of the saved, both dead and alive, will be resurrected. This is the main harvest.

For this we say unto you by the word of the Lord, that we which are alive and remain unto the coming of the Lord shall not prevent them which are asleep. For the Lord himself shall descend from heaven with a shout, with the voice of the archangel, and with the trump of God: and the dead in Christ shall rise first: Then we which are alive and remain shall be caught up together with them in the clouds, to meet

the Lord in the air: and so shall we ever be with the Lord.
1 Thessalonians 4:15-17

To help you see this, I have included a little chart. I said the harvest is prophetic in nature. The harvest is only for the saved. The lost are not harvested and do not go to be with the Lord. They are the *"tares"* that are with the wheat and get sifted out. The harvest is in three stages as shown below. There are two resurrections. One for the saved and one for the lost. The resurrection of the saved is in three stages. The resurrection of the bodies of the lost is in one stage at the Great White Throne judgment. See the chart below. I think this will be a help to you.

Resurrection of the Saved (First Resurrection)	Resurrection of the Lost (Second Resurrection)
In Three Stages **1. Firstfruits: Calvary** Matthew 27:50-53 I Corinthians 15:17-26 **2. Main Harvest: Rapture** Revelation 4:1 I Thessalonians 4:16 I Corinthians 15:51-52 **3. Gleanings: Second Coming** Revelation 14:14-17 Note: You can liken this to three stages of harvesting a crop.	Great White Throne Revelation 20:4-5 at end of 1000 year Millennium. All who are resurrected at this time are lost.

Parable of the Ten Virgins
Matthew 25:1-13
1 Then shall the kingdom of heaven be likened unto ten virgins, which took their lamps, and went forth to meet the bridegroom.
2 And five of them were wise, and five were foolish.
3 They that were foolish took their lamps, and took no oil

147

with them:

4 But the wise took oil in their vessels with their lamps.

5 While the bridegroom tarried, they all slumbered and slept.

6 And at midnight there was a cry made, Behold, the bridegroom cometh; go ye out to meet him.

7 Then all those virgins arose, and trimmed their lamps.

8 And the foolish said unto the wise, Give us of your oil; for our lamps are gone out.

9 But the wise answered, saying, Not so; lest there be not enough for us and you: but go ye rather to them that sell, and buy for yourselves.

10 And while they went to buy, the bridegroom came; and they that were ready went in with him to the marriage: and the door was shut.

11 Afterward came also the other virgins, saying, Lord, Lord, open to us.

12 But he answered and said, Verily I say unto you, I know you not.

13 Watch therefore, for ye know neither the day nor the hour wherein the Son of man cometh.

In Chapter 2 of this book we looked at the customs of the Jewish wedding and how they were patterned after the Biblical truths of the Lord coming to claim His bride at the rapture. As you know, Matthew Chapter 24 is a prophetic chapter that is mainly speaking to Israel. Many get confused because they do not understand this and most folks that preach a post-tribulation rapture do so because they get confused in Matthew 24.

The parable of the ten virgins is the first of three parables given in Matthew 25. The purpose of these three parables is to shed more light on the end-time events just discussed in Chapter 24. We will not look at the other two, though they are prophetic as well. We are going to look at the prophetic lessons taught in the parable of the ten virgins.

1. The ten virgins are a type of the church that exists right before the Lord comes.

2. The Bridegroom is the Lord Jesus Christ.

3. In verse 2 we see that there were five wise and five foolish. Fifty percent of the church is living very foolishly, we can certainly see that can't we?

4. In verse 3, we see that only five virgins had oil for their lamps. Oil is a type of the Holy Spirit and seems to signify that five of the ten were not saved.

5. Half of the people in your average church right before the Lord returns are lost. What a sad and sobering thought that is.

6. According to verse 5, all ten virgins slumbered and slept. That means not only are half the people in our churches unsaved, but even those who are saved are not watching and waiting for the Bridegroom to return. How about you, my friend? Are you born again? Are you saved? If you have been saved, are you busy for the Lord? Will He find you watching and waiting when He returns? This passage haunts me. It indicates that very few people today are walking with the Lord.

One of these days, according to this passage, the Lord Jesus Christ is going to come for us. The trumpet shall sound in Heaven and a shout will be made at your door. It is possible that only half the people in your church will be taken and of those who are saved, they will be found not watching and not ready to stand in the presence of the Lord. According to verse 9, you can not share the oil. Every man must trust in the Lord for himself. Your children and grandchildren can not go to Heaven on your coat tails. They must get their own oil by trusting in the Lord Jesus Christ. They must accept His wedding proposal for themselves. In verses 10-12 we see that if a person misses the rapture, the door is shut, just as the door of the ark was shut in Noah's day. If you had an opportunity to be saved but rejected it, you will not get a second chance.

First Coming of Christ was a shadow.

The first Coming of Christ was a shadow of the Second Coming of Christ. <u>Jesus came in two stages just like the second coming is in two stages.</u> He came first as a baby born in a manger. It was a very quiet event unknown to most. At the age of thirty he was baptized of John in the Jordan and began His ministry. The second time He is coming secretly to meet us in the air at the rapture. After the seven-year Tribulation He comes back publicly on a white horse and *"every eye shall see Him."*

Let me give you a few shadows we can glean from the first coming of Christ that point to the conditions of things at His second coming.

1. It was a time of tyrannical <u>dictatorship</u>. Luke 2:1

Taxes, debt and oppression were common. In fact God used the greed of Caesar and taxes to fulfill prophecy. It was for this purpose that Joseph and Mary were in Bethlehem when Jesus was born. We live in a similar time period today.

2. He came the first time to a generation of people who had <u>no room</u> for Him. Luke 2:7

He will soon return for a church that has no room for Him.

3. He came in the <u>darkness</u> of night. Luke 2:9

He is coming again the second time into the darkness of sin and shame. He is coming to a church filled with fornication, adulteries, and filth. He is coming to the Laodicean church. This is the church that has lost all

150

boundaries and erased all lines of separation. This is the big one size fits all, come as you are and be happy church. It is worth noting here that the first six churches are called "the church in Ephesus," "the church in Smyrna," and so on. But look how this last church is addressed: *And unto the angel of the church of the Laodiceans write; These things saith the Amen, the faithful and true witness, the beginning of the creation of God; (Revelation 3:14)*

This is the church that is prophetic of the last Church Age, the one we are living in now. The Lord seems to be revealing that the church has become a big all inclusive universal assembly in the last days rather than a place for Spirit-filled saints separated unto God.

4. He came upon a generation that was <u>unaware</u>. Matthew 2

When the wise men showed up at the temple looking for the King of the Jews, they found a people who were completely unaware. I believe your average child of God today is unaware. We really do not think the Lord is coming soon. Most preachers are scoffers when it comes to prophecy.

5. He came at a time of famine of the word of God.

Amos 8 :11 Behold, the days come, saith the Lord GOD, that I will send a famine in the land, not a famine of bread, nor a thirst for water, but of hearing the words of the LORD:

For four hundred years there had been very little communication with the Lord. There are four hundred years between Malachi and Matthew. Then God sent Jesus, the Word of God, into the world. Friend, today it is the same. We have new versions of the Bible written every year; words are changed, and whole verses are taken out. People are confused about where to find the truth. Did you know that the King James 1611 Bible turned four hundred years old just a short time back? Does that mean anything? Could the living Word of God be about to return?

151

Observations

1. God communes with the humble. At the birth of Christ, God did not go to the palace, He met with lowly shepherds.
2. Don't let the Lord find you unaware at His coming!
3. Get an urgency about the things of God and the return of Christ.

You know, when Christ came in that first stage as a baby, not much changed in the world. He walked the earth for thirty years before His ministry started and almost nobody knew He was here. <u>I have a feeling that after the rapture, which is the first stage of His second coming, that not many are going to be aware that we are even gone.</u> Apart from the terrible things that take place during the Tribulation, few will have any knowledge that the Lord has come.

A Shadow is a Cloudy Replica of the Real Thing

THE VEIL THAT SEPARATES
THE OLD FROM THE NEW
Chapter 14

Several years ago I was speaking on the phone to a preacher friend named Bill Waugh. We were talking about prophecy, which is what we usually talk about. Together we learned some pretty important truths about the return of the Lord and as a team we came up with some pieces of the puzzle that so many have missed over the years. We even wrote a book together called "A Seven-Fold Promise of His Soon Coming." One of the pieces to the puzzle came as a result of this phone call. As we were discussing prophecy, I made the declaration that I did not believe the New Testament started at the birth of Christ, but rather at the death of Christ. There was dead silence on the phone as my friend began to digest the consequences of this statement. I remember him saying, "Dan, don't tell me that, this means we have 33 more years!" In other words, I just added 33 more years to be fulfilled to make up the 2000 year New Testament Age. I remember we talked some more and then hung up. It was several hours later when the phone rang and Pastor Waugh had come up with a notion that God uses a 360 day year rather than our 365 ¼ day solar year like we use. We began doing the math and decided that we are in fact getting close to the 2000th year of the Church Age. It is complicated. The calendar has been messed with over the years. Nobody really knows the exact date of Calvary, so it is something we will never be able to pin down for sure. I think the Lord planned it that way. I believe there are 4000 years in the Old Testament and 2000 years in the New Testament. I have already shared this with you in a previous chapter. However, if this is true, it is pretty important that we begin the New Testament at the right time. Since Jesus lived 33 ½ years, it becomes quite important in determining the start of the New Testament. I have also come to the conclusion that to measure years, you have to use the same calculator that God uses. God always uses a 360 day prophetic year. We use a 365 ¼ day year. The Jews use a 354 2/3rd day lunar year. See the mess and confusion that we have to deal with to figure this out? Let me see if I can clear up some of the confusion concerning the different calendars.

The cycles of the sun and moon do not synchronize well. (Probably a result of the curse upon the world itself after the fall of Lucifer and man, or a result of the flood in Noah's day). A lunar year is 354 2/3rd days in length while a solar year is 365 ¼ days. Almost exactly in the middle is the prophetic 360 day year. The number 360 is interesting for several reasons. There are 360 degrees in a perfect circle. There are 360 degrees on a compass. It is the sum of the angles of a four-sided object. It is the perfect number a perfect God uses to mark a prophetic year. I believe that at creation, the earth had perfect days of 12 hours of night and 12 hours of day. I believe the earth also had a perfect 360 day year. Sin had not corrupted things yet; the earth was a paradise.

Let's look at some reasons we should not use the solar calendar in our prophetic studies. By solar, I mean the 365 ¼ day calendar we use today in America.

What's wrong with our calendar?
1. Consider who gave us the current calendar we use today.

It was not Bible believing people, but rather the Romans with their belief in the sun god and many other heathen practices who gave us our calendar. It has been revised several times over the years, but the sun, not the moon, has been the premise.

2. Consider the people who have used the sun (solstices, equinoxes, and eclipses, etc...) to measure their years and mark pagan and religious holidays.

Egyptians, Babylonians, Persians, Romans, Druids, Celts, Inca, Mayan, Aztecs, and others either worshiped the sun or the sun gods and marked their years by its position. None of these groups were ever accused of being Bible believing soul winners, to say the least.

3. Consider that a prophetic year is 360 days not 365 ¼ days and based on the moon not the sun.

God uses the moon, not the sun to measure months and prophetic years. He speaks of 42 months as the last half of the seven-year Tribulation, which is three and a half years. This is found in (Revelation 13:5) *And there was given unto him a mouth speaking great things and blasphemies; and power was given unto him to continue forty and two months.*

The entire Hebrew calendar is based on the moon. Each of their months start on the new moon. The Revelation speaks of the second half of the Tribulation as 1,260 days. When you do the math, you find that is three and a half years of 360 days each. I believe at creation, the world was perfect and it took exactly 360 days for the earth to travel around the sun. Before the curse, the solar and lunar calendars were synchronized. A perfect God would not have a 365 ¼ day year, would He? After the curse, things changed and now it is out of order.

(Genesis 1:14-16) *And God said, Let there be lights in the firmament of the heaven to divide the day from the night; and let them be for signs, and for seasons, and for days, and years: And let them be for lights in the firmament of the heaven to give light upon the earth: and it was so. And God made two great lights; the greater light to rule the day, and the lesser light to rule the night: he made the stars also.*

God made the sun, moon, and the stars during the creative week. Besides giving light, they also are for determining signs and seasons. For example, Isaiah and Revelation, as well as the book of Joel, Matthew and others, all talk about the signs in the moon and sun concerning the last days. He speaks of the moon turning to blood before the second coming. God uses the sun and the moon for signs, but God uses the 360-day year for His prophetic calendar. The nation of Israel has always been under a lunar-based calendar, not the Roman calendar we use.

(Psalms 104:19) He appointed the moon for seasons: the sun knoweth his going down.

(Psalms 89:37) It shall be established for ever as the moon, and as a faithful witness in heaven. Selah.

God uses the moon, not the sun, as an example of a faithful witness.

(Psalms 81:3) Blow up the trumpet in the new moon, in the time appointed, on our solemn feast day.

This is probably speaking of the Feast of Trumpets, which begins on the first day of Tishri, which is their seventh month. Remember, their months always started on the new moon. All I am saying is that Israel always used a 360-day lunar, not solar calendar.

Take note of the following verses, which all speak of 1,260 days making up a three and a half year period of time during the Tribulation. These are all in reference to a 360 day year. Our 365 ¼ day calendar will not fit.

(Revelation 11:3) *And I will give power unto my two witnesses, and they shall prophesy a thousand two hundred and threescore days, clothed in sackcloth.*

Speaking of the first half (3 1/2 years) of the Tribulation. (Revelation 12:6) *And the woman fled into the*

wilderness, where she hath a place prepared of God, that
they should feed her there a thousand two hundred and
threescore days.

This is speaking of the second 3 ½ years of the tribulation.

4. Our Gregorian (solar calendar) has a number of weaknesses.

It cannot be divided into equal halves or quarters. There are different numbers of days per month, and the months or years may begin on any day of the week. Recent discoveries have also revealed that changes in the rotation of the earth (massive earthquakes) and changes in the earth's orbit around the sun affect the length of a day in hours and minutes. Since the sun is burning, it is constantly shrinking; causing the time it takes the earth to revolve around it to change slightly. Sound confusing? It is. Nobody will ever be able to prove exactly what year it is on God's prophetic calendar. God has ordained it that way. "*No man knows the day or the hour*!"

5. The solar calendar started at the wrong time!

If you have a Scofield Bible, you will see a date at the top of each page. A Bishop named James Ussher came up with these dates. He meant well, and I am sure he was acting on the information available to him back in the 1600's, but he has the Old Testament ending at the birth of Christ. In fact, he has Jesus being born in 4 B.C. Isn't that interesting? Jesus was born four years before Jesus. Now, we all fell into this false teaching didn't we? We all have bought in to the belief that the New Testament started at the birth of Jesus Christ. Problem is, it is just not the truth. The New Testament began when Christ died on Calvary and the veil of the temple was rent in two. We see this clearly in Daniel Chapter 9.

(Daniel 9:24-26) *Seventy weeks are determined upon thy*
people and upon thy holy city, to finish the transgression,
and to make an end of sins, and to make reconciliation for

iniquity, and to bring in everlasting righteousness, and to seal up the vision and prophecy, and to anoint the most Holy. Know therefore and understand, that from the going forth of the commandment to restore and to build Jerusalem unto the Messiah the Prince shall be seven weeks, and threescore and two weeks: the street shall be built again, and the wall, even in troublous times. And after threescore and two weeks shall Messiah be cut off, but not for himself: and the people of the prince that shall come shall destroy the city and the sanctuary; and the end thereof shall be with a flood, and unto the end of the war desolations are determined.

Notice what I underlined in the verses above. The Bible clearly states that seventy weeks (490 years) are determined upon Israel. The 69th week, which is Old Testament, did not end at the birth of Christ, but at Calvary when Messiah was "cut off" as the text shows. My friend, as you can see in the passage above, Daniel's 70th week (seven-year Tribulation) is also Old Testament! We also see this in,

(Hebrews 9:14-18) *How much more shall the blood of Christ, who through the eternal Spirit offered himself without spot to God, purge your conscience from dead works to serve the living God? And for this cause he is the mediator of the new testament, that by means of death, for the redemption of the transgressions that were under the first testament, they which are called might receive the promise of eternal inheritance. For where a testament is, there must also of necessity be the death of the testator. For a testament is of force after men are dead: otherwise it is of no strength at all while the testator liveth. Whereupon neither the first testament was dedicated without blood.*

Any court of law would tell you that a will is not binding until the death of the person. Webster's 1828 Dictionary defines a Testator as:

TESTA'TOR, n. [L.] A man who makes and leaves a will or testament

158

at death.

The New Testament could not have begun until Christ went to the cross.

In closing this chapter, please consider these further proofs that the New Testament could not have begun until after the cross and the renting of the veil in the temple as was so elegantly written by Pastor Bill Waugh with some not so elegant aid from me:

WHEN DID THE
NEW TESTAMENT BEGIN
By Pastor Bill Waugh
&
Evangelist Dan Goodwin

January 2000 found a number of Christians wondering if this would be the year of Christ's return. Many were "packing up" spiritually speaking by expecting the rapture while others were "stocking up" for the Y2K crisis that never was. Some were under the impression Jesus would surely come after two-thousand years of the New Testament Age but as we will see, it was not the two-thousandth year of the New Testament Age after all.

(Psalms 90:12) So teach us to number our days, that we may apply our hearts unto wisdom.

If one were to attempt to number the days or years of the New Testament Age, would we start at the birth of Christ, His baptism, or His death? When did the New Testament Age begin? I believe the New Testament Age began not at the birth of Christ, but rather at Calvary. Let me give you several reasons why I strongly believe this.

1. THE OBSERVANCE OF THE SABBATH.

From the time of Moses, through the entire earthly life of

159

Christ, the Sabbath was observed. Jesus, our example, always honored the Sabbath day, visited the synagogues, and observed the feast days. Does this sound like the New Testament Age to you? Not until after His death, burial, and resurrection did Christians gather on the first day of the week after the example of the Apostles. The Old Testament was spent laboring six days then resting on the Sabbath. Christ paid the sin debt at Calvary and we have already entered into His rest (Hebrews Chapter 4). Praise the Lord! Now for nearly two-thousand years, we gather on Sunday, the Lord's Day, and labor for Him the rest of the week because we are already eternally saved!

2. THE SACRIFICES

The Old Testament sacrifices were being offered throughout the earthly life of our Saviour. Christ even died on the Eve of Passover (Nisan 14), the same day the lambs were being slain. Does observing the Old Testament sacrifices sound like a New Testament doctrine to you? Christ became our sacrifice at Calvary thus ending the need to picture His death by the slaying of animals.

(Hebrews 10:10-12) *By the which will we are sanctified through the offering of the body of Jesus Christ once for all. And every priest standeth daily ministering and offering oftentimes the same sacrifices, which can never take away sins: But this man, after he had offered one sacrifice for sins for ever, sat down on the right hand of God;*

3. THE VEIL OF THE TEMPLE

(Matthew 27:50-51) *Jesus, when he had cried again with a loud voice, yielded up the ghost. And, behold, the veil of the temple was rent in twain from the top to the bottom; and the earth did quake, and the rocks rent;*

The veil in the temple was not rent in twain until after Jesus died. This veil was a barrier between God and man and could only be passed through by a High Priest. This veil was no longer needed because Jesus, who became our sacrifice, had just become our High Priest. At the very moment of His death, our Saviour cried out, "It is finished." He was speaking of three things:

1. His physical life.
2. The payment for sin.
3. Old Testament Age.

Would the New Testament Age have begun before the veil of the temple was torn from top to bottom? The answer is no.

Wherefore remember, that ye being in time past Gentiles in the flesh, who are called Uncircumcision by that which is called the Circumcision in the flesh made by hands; That at that time ye were without Christ, being aliens from the commonwealth of Israel, and strangers from the covenants of promise, having no hope, and without God in the world: But now in Christ Jesus ye who sometimes were far off are made nigh by the blood of Christ. For he is our peace, who hath made both one, and hath broken down the middle wall of partition between us; Having abolished in his flesh the enmity, even the law of commandments contained in ordinances; for to make in himself of twain one new man, so making peace; And that he might reconcile both unto God in one body by the cross, having slain the enmity thereby: And came and preached peace to you which were afar off, and to them that were nigh. For through him we both have access by one Spirit unto the Father. (Ephesians 2:11-18)

4. THE DEATH OF THE TESTATOR

(Hebrews 9:15-17) And for this cause he is the mediator of the new testament, that by means of death, for the redemption of the transgressions that were under the first testament, they which are called might receive the promise of eternal inheritance. For where a testament is, there must also of necessity be the death of the testator. For a testament

is of force after men are dead: otherwise it is of no strength at all while the testator liveth.

If a man were to record his last will and testament, an interesting thing takes place. A promise and certain conditions are made and are considered legal but not binding until a very important event takes place, the death of the testator. Christ is the Lamb slain from the foundation of the world. This was sealed in the foreknowledge of God. At the cross of Calvary the Testator died for the sins of the world and the New Testament Age began.

See some definitions from Webster's 1828:

TESTA'TOR, n. [L.] A man who makes and leaves a will or testament at death.

TEST'AMENT, n. [L. testamentum, from testor, to make a will.]
1. A solemn authentic instrument in writing, by which a person declares his will as to the disposal of his estate and effects after his death. This is otherwise called a will. A testament, to be valid, must be made when the testator is of sound mind, and it must be subscribed, witnessed and published in such manner as the law prescribes.
A man in certain cases may make a valid will by words only, and such will is called nuncupative.
2. The name of each general division of the canonical books of the sacred Scriptures; as the Old Testament; the New Testament. The name is equivalent to covenant, and in our use of it, we apply it to the books, which contain the old and new dispensations; that of Moses, and that of Jesus Christ.

5. THE OLD TESTAMENT SAINTS

(Ephesians 4:7-10) *But unto every one of us is given grace according to the measure of the gift of Christ. Wherefore he saith, When he ascended up on high, he led captivity captive, and gave gifts unto men. (Now that he ascended, what is it but that he also descended first into the lower parts of the earth? He that descended is the same also that ascended up far above all heavens, that he might fill all things.)*

162

There are two examples in the Bible about saints who died and went to Paradise. One example is seen in Luke Chapter 16. Lazarus died and was *"carried by the angels into Abraham's bosom."* Another time is the thief on the cross who trusted Jesus and was told by Christ; *"Today thou shalt be with me in paradise. "* (See Luke 23:43) Once the New Testament Age begins, every saint who dies is absent from the body and present with the Lord.

2 Corinthians 5:8

We are confident, I say, and willing rather to be absent from the body, and to be present with the Lord.

There is an obvious difference in what happens at death before the cross in relation to what happens at the death of a saint after the cross.

***Contact me for a booklet I have written called "ABRAHAM'S BOSOM" that gives great detail about Old Testament salvation and why they did not go to Heaven.

6. DANIEL'S 69 WEEKS OF PROPHECY

(Daniel 9:24-26) Seventy weeks are determined upon thy people and upon thy holy city, to finish the transgression, and to make an end of sins, and to make reconciliation for iniquity, and to bring in everlasting righteousness, and to seal up the vision and prophecy, and to anoint the most Holy. Know therefore and understand, that from the going forth of the commandment to restore and to build Jerusalem unto the Messiah the Prince shall be seven weeks, and threescore and two weeks: the street shall be built again, and the wall, even in troublous times. And after threescore and two weeks shall Messiah be cut off, but not for himself: and the people of the prince that shall come shall destroy the city and the sanctuary; and the end thereof shall be with a flood, and unto the end of the war desolations are determined.

Daniel's 69 weeks (483 years) were counting down from the time of Nehemiah until Christ, the Messiah, was cut off at Calvary. The ending of this prophetic countdown was not the birth of Christ but rather the death of Christ on the cross. After the New Testament Age ends with the rapture of the saints, Daniel's seventieth week (the Tribulation period) begins. This seventieth week completes the prophecy of Daniel Chapter 9, and finishes off four thousand years of the Old Testament. Bishop Ussher, from the 1600's, meant well when he put 4 B.C. for the date of the birth of Christ. He was simply trying to make the dates agree with the Roman solar calendar, but **nobody can understand prophecy as clearly as the generation living right before Christ comes for us!**

Listen to what Scofield said in his introduction to The Revelation; **"Doubtless much which is designedly obscure to us will be clear to those for whom it was written as the time approaches."**

Please note this section is called, *When did the New Testament Begin*. It does not say *When did the Church begin*. Christ is the head of the church that was started during His earthly ministry when He called out the twelve. Christ is the Chief Cornerstone, the Apostles are the foundation and we are built on them. (Ephesians 2:20-22)
And are built upon the foundation of the apostles and prophets, Jesus Christ himself being the chief corner stone; In whom all the building fitly framed together groweth unto an holy temple in the Lord: In whom ye also are builded together for an habitation of God through the Spirit.

Just as in a normal physical birth, the head appears first followed by the rest of the body. Christ the head appeared first and the apostles and disciples followed. The rest of the church is built upon this foundation. A physical birth also includes a separation and cutting of the cord followed by the breath of life. Interestingly, after Christ paid the sin debt dying for our sins He later ascended (separation) and the church breathed the breath of life (the Holy Spirit indwelling each believer) in the upper room and at Pentecost. The church was clearly in existence several years before Calvary and the beginning of the New Testament Age.

This is so simple yet many have missed it for centuries. I believe it is possible that this is part of the sealing up of the book as Daniel was told. Maybe this has been revealed in these last days to sound one last warning to the people of God to prepare for the Lord's soon return! Are you ready?

Verily I say unto you, This generation shall not pass, till all these things be fulfilled.
(Matthew 24:34)

THE LAST GENERATION
Chapter 15

Verily I say unto you, This generation shall not pass, till all these things be fulfilled.
Matthew 24:34

Someone is going to be alive when the trumpet sounds. Someone is going to be the final generation upon this earth. Have you ever thought about that? Have you ever wondered if we could be that last generation? If you were reasonably sure that we were that final generation, would it have an effect on you? Would you make any changes in your life? Would you set some different goals and seek to do more for the Lord?

I am going to give you several reasons why I believe we may in fact be that final generation. Some of these reasons we have already discussed, but we are going to look at this from a different angle. You see, there are certain things that have to be in place when the saints are removed and the Tribulation takes place. There is a system that must be in place, a mindset that must be in play. **The final generation on the earth right before the trumpet sounds has got to be ready to move rapidly into the events that unfold during the Tribulation.** I believe we are that final generation. I believe the world is ready to move into this one-world system controlled by Antichrist. The only thing holding it back is the saints who are indwelled by the Holy Ghost.

(2 Thessalonians 2:1-8) Now we beseech you, brethren, by the coming of our Lord Jesus Christ, and by our gathering together unto him, That ye be not soon shaken in mind, or be

troubled, neither by spirit, nor by word, nor by letter as from us, as that the day of Christ is at hand. Let no man deceive you by any means: for that day shall not come, except there come a falling away first, and that man of sin be revealed, the son of perdition; Who opposeth and exalteth himself above all that is called God, or that is worshipped; so that he as God sitteth in the temple of God, shewing himself that he is God. Remember ye not, that, when I was yet with you, I told you these things? And now ye know what withholdeth that he might be revealed in his time. For the mystery of iniquity doth already work: only he who now letteth will let, until he be taken out of the way. And then shall that Wicked be revealed, whom the Lord shall consume with the spirit of his mouth, and shall destroy with the brightness of his coming:

I believe all things are in place and ready for the man of sin to be revealed. I believe you and I are living in this LAST GENERATION that is alive right before the trumpet sounds.

The following are my reasons why I strongly believe this.

1. Our generation has made it possible for one man to effectively rule the whole world.

Through the technology of computers, satellite, phones, and the ease and speed of travel, one man could actually rule the whole world from a remote location somewhere. We know from Revelation 6 that the Antichrist will rule the world after we are gone. Already it is plain to see that this is possible. Our President, from the comfort of the Oval Office, simply gives the word and a drone can take out a rogue leader on the other side of the ocean. Our President can pretty much communicate any message he chooses and it will be transmitted around the globe. He can pick up the Blackberry he carries and speak to any world leader he chooses at the drop of a hat. Never before has a generation been capable of these things like it is in our day. The generation on the scene when the Lord returns has to be able to operate under a one-world dictator. It is plain that we fit that qualification today. The whole world is ready for this one-world leader to come on the scene. The world is already connected globally. The financial markets, commerce, airlines, credit cards, all are connected together. Even EBAY is global! Never before has there been a time when the one-world order is in place and ready as it is today.

2. Our generation has the ability to destroy the world.

Mark 13:20 makes it clear that at the final battle at the end of the seven-year Tribulation, the nations would have destroyed themselves unless Christ had shortened the days. *And except that the Lord had shortened those days, no flesh should be saved: but for the elect's sake, whom he hath chosen, he hath shortened the days.*

This passage has some other interesting lessons to teach us as well, but regardless, it certainly shows that the world is hanging by a thread during the final months. Here are some facts about the status of the world we live in right now. Military experts say that Russia right now has 10,000 ICBM's aimed at the United States of America. Each one of these intercontinental ballistic missiles is more powerful than the bombs dropped on Japan in 1945! From the time the button is pushed, it takes about 15 minutes to reach its target here in America. If even half of them make it through, America would cease to exist! Several small nations around the world have joined the ranks with nuclear weapons. North Korea has nukes. Iran is very close to having nukes. Pakistan has nukes. Israel has nukes. It would not take much for a worldwide nuclear war to break out. America is believed to have bombs that are so powerful they have not even been tested! Notice in the first four seals of Revelation

6 that 1/4th of the world's population will die as a result of war. That is around 1 billion souls! Never before has a generation had such a destructive capability. The world is more unstable today than it has ever been in history. The world has the ability to bring total destruction upon itself. Just look at the disaster that has come and is yet to come, from the nuclear power plant in Japan. They say that radiation is just now coming to the Pacific shores of California. This stuff is nothing to play with. I believe 1000's and 1000's will be effected by that reactor, and that is just a drop in the bucket compared to a nuclear war!

*** I read this somewhere; I cannot remember where. I read that one nuclear submarine today has more fire power than all the bombs dropped in WWII by BOTH sides! Let that sink in for a minute. I am simply saying that our generation is capable of destroying the world and therefore fits the description of the generation that goes into the Tribulation. You and I had better get ready for the return of the Lord!

3. Our generation has witnessed the arrival of the Global society through supersonic travel and the availability of almost unlimited knowledge.

(Daniel 12:4) But thou, O Daniel, shut up the words, and seal the book, even to the time of the end: <u>many shall run to and fro, and knowledge shall be increased</u>.

It is frightening when you think how fast the access of knowledge is since the computer came about. In addition, every year they are smarter, faster, and easier to use. And now they are more portable than ever. Just look around next time you go out in public, everyone is looking down at a hand held device and are connected globally to the world by way of a smart phone. These are developments that will be necessary for the Antichrist when he takes over the world. Add to that the ability to travel the world at supersonic speeds. The truth is, a person no longer has to physically travel any more. By way of the internet you can travel just about anywhere in the world. The Antichrist will use modern technology to communicate and be seen by people around the globe. Think about that next time you read this Scripture: *(Revelation 13:13-14) And he doeth great wonders, so that he maketh fire come down from heaven on the earth <u>in the sight of men</u>, And deceiveth them that dwell on the earth by the means of those miracles which he had power to do in the sight of the beast; saying to them that dwell on the earth, that they should make an image to the beast, which had the wound by a sword, and did live.*

4. Our generation has excelled in its apathy.

There has always been evil. Every generation has had its sinners and evil doers, but it seems like this generation has perfected not only evil, but the ignorance of evil.

(2 Timothy 3:1-5) This know also, that in the last days perilous times shall come. For men shall be lovers of their own selves, covetous, boasters, proud, blasphemers, disobedient to parents, unthankful, unholy, Without natural affection, trucebreakers, false accusers, incontinent, fierce, despisers of those that are good, Traitors, heady, highminded, lovers of pleasures more than lovers of God; Having a form of godliness, but denying the power thereof: from such turn away.

Just take a look at that description by Paul of how things will be in the last generation. Tell me that isn't us! There are so many things I could share that are going on today, terrible and evil things. But my point is not in reference to the evil being propagated by our generation. My point is in reference to the way that **we have perfected the art of ignoring the evil that is around us**. Let me just give one example that kind of sums up this generation. I want to warn you, this is a very graphic description of the atrocities carried out by an abortion doctor right here in the "Christian" nation we call America. I have three grandchildren. Two of them I have held in my arms when they were just hours old. I have to tell you, the following news article is hard for me to read. I am giving you fair warning ahead of time. You may want to turn the page. I give this story to prove my point. America and the world have perfected evil beyond any generation I have ever studied, including the evil of Hitler! Much of what is described in this story is going on in abortion clinics all over America! No wonder we would rather not know, and would rather bury our heads in the sand! To know is to be accountable, to do something to stop it!

Philadelphia abortion clinic horror:
April 11, 2013 USA Today

Infant beheadings. Severed baby feet in jars. A child screaming after it was delivered alive during an abortion procedure. Haven't heard about these sickening accusations?

It's not your fault. Since the murder trial of Pennsylvania abortion doctor Kermit Gosnell began March 18, there has been precious little coverage of the case that should be on every news show and front page. The revolting revelations of Gosnell's former staff, who have been testifying to what they witnessed and did during late-term abortions, should shock anyone with a heart.

NBC-10 Philadelphia reported that, Stephen Massof, a former Gosnell worker, "described how he snipped the spinal cords of babies, calling it, 'literally a beheading. It is separating the brain from the body." One former worker, Adrienne Moton, testified that Gosnell taught her his "snipping" technique to use on infants born alive.

Massof, who, like other witnesses, has himself pleaded guilty to serious crimes, testified "It would rain fetuses. Fetuses and blood all over the place." Here is the headline the Associated Press put on a story about his testimony that he saw 100 babies born and then snipped: "Staffer describes chaos at PA abortion clinic."

"Chaos" isn't really the story here. Butchering babies that were already born and were older than the state's 24-week limit for abortions is the story. There is a reason the late Democratic senator Daniel Patrick Moynihan called this procedure infanticide.

www.usatoday.com/story/opinion/2013/04/10/philadelphia-abortion-clinic-horror-column/2072577/

That is not the whole story, but it is more than enough! What a sickening and evil generation! But do you know what is worse? The fact that the whole country including the news media, the average church, and the population in general, have tried to ignore this story. No doubt some of you reading this book have just heard about the trial I mentioned for the very first time. America is guilty of murdering babies since 1973. At least that is the year the Supreme Court told us it was ok to murder babies in the mother's womb. What took place at this clinic is probably going on in many other clinics, but America has so much guilt and blood on her hands she refuses to even face her shame. America has tried to hide from this story. The media ignored it as much as they could. Congress has ignored it, the state of Pennsylvania where this took place wishes the story would go away. Most churches would rather not know about the reality of abortion. Do you know why? **Because as a nation, we are guilty!** This is a crime against little babies. This is a crime against life. This is a crime against God. Every single person in America carries some of the blame and guilt for this terrible evil that is going on. In Hitler's day, much of the world turned their back and tried to ignore the Holocaust. Many tried to deny that anything so tragic could be happening. In fact, some still deny it today. America since 1973 is doing the same thing. In recent years I think the denial is not just from the world but from God's people as well. The church has turned her back and refuses to acknowledge the extermination of one million precious souls each year. While sitting at my desk writing this it was quite shocking to see the following headline in today's news:

I Am Overwhelmed by 55 Million Babies Killed Since Roe v. Wade
by Kristan Hawkins | Washington, DC | LifeNews.com | 1/22/13
http://www.lifenews.com/2013/01/22/i-am-overwhelmed-by-55-million-babies-killed-since-roe-v-wade/

This is a story showing that 55 million babies have been murdered since 1973. May the Lord have mercy on us for standing by and allowing this to take place. That story is a year old. The number is now over 56 million. The murder of these millions of babies is a far worse "Holocaust" than what happened to the Jews.

Consider the following newsletter from Chuck Baldwin dated1-23-14:

Yesterday marked the 41st anniversary of the infamous US Supreme Court Roe v. Wade decision, which, in effect, legalized abortion-on-demand nationwide. The aftermath of this tragic ruling is the deaths of over 55 million innocent unborn babies. It is no hyperbole to say abortion-on-demand is America's national holocaust. Think about it, every American citizen today, 41 years old or younger, has never known a country that respected and protected innocent human life in the womb.

Consider this, too: when Hitler's Third Reich was at its zenith, the abortion rate in Germany was 40%. Guess what? The abortion rate in America today is right at 40%. In fact, statistically speaking, the most dangerous place to be in America is not in an automobile without wearing a seat belt, or on a commercial airliner with a potential terrorist on board, but in the womb of one's mother.

What is especially irritating about the whole abortion debate is the way the subject has been used as a political football by those on both the right and the left of the political aisle. While the national Democratic Party proudly touts itself as being "pro-choice," it has been the so-called "pro-life" Republican Party that is mostly to blame for legalized abortion being left as the law of the land for over four decades.

Think of it: the GOP has dominated US Supreme Court appointments for the 41 years since the Roe decision. In fact, the 1973 court that released the Roe decision was a Republican-appointed court by a 6-3 margin. The same GOP-dominated court also rendered the Doe v. Bolton Supreme Court decision reaffirming Roe. Consider still: the "pro-life" Republican Party controlled the entire federal government from the election of 2000 to the election of 2006: six long years of GOP domination of both houses

174

of Congress, the White House, and the US Supreme Court. And in all of that time, not one single unborn baby's life was saved. Not one! And, yet, each year, former Congressman Ron Paul (R-TX) would introduce the Sanctity of Life Act. And each year, the bill would sit in the document room of the Capitol Building and gather dust. What would Rep. Paul's bill have done? (1) It would have defined unborn babies as persons under the law. (2) Under the authority of Article. III. Section. 2. of the US Constitution, it would have removed abortion from the jurisdiction of the court. Had the "pro-life" Republican congress passed Dr. Paul's bill, and the "pro-life" President, G. W. Bush, signed it into law, Roe v. Wade would have been effectively overturned. So, why didn't President Bush trumpet the bill? Where was the Republican leader in the Senate? Where was the Republican Speaker of the House? Where was Orrin Hatch? Where was John McCain? Where was Lindsey Graham? Where was the National Right to Life Committee? Where were the tens of thousands of "pro-life" pastors and Christians? I remind you that securing life and liberty is the primary purpose of government (read the Declaration of Independence). Should it surprise us that the same government that feels no responsibility to protect the lives of innocent unborn children would feel any responsibility to protect our liberties? No wonder this government seems hell-bent on destroying our personal liberties: the wanton slaughter of 55 million unborn babies has seared its conscience. Worse yet is the manner in which our pastors and churches seem completely unsympathetic to the silent screams of the slaughtered unborn. Legalized abortion is a national holocaust; an affront to our national character; a contradiction of established principles subscribed to from the beginning of Western Civilization; an insult to the principles of our Declaration of Independence; a bane of our national spirit; and a stench in the nostrils of Almighty God that we have allowed it to continue for 41 years now stands as an indictment against this generation of Americans (especially America's Christians) and bodes ominously for the well-being of our posterity.

Chuck Baldwin
January 23, 2014
NewsWithViews.com

Just last night I held Chloe, my little granddaughter, in my arms. She is just a few weeks old. She is very precious to our family, as are all of our grandchildren. There are over 56 million precious little ones just like our Chloe that never made it to their mother's arms! It brings chills down my back and a sickness in my stomach to imagine the abortion doctor taking the life away from a precious little baby. When I think of a mother granting permission for a "doctor" to come in and destroy this human being inside her womb, this miracle of God; it leaves me with no words to describe what I feel. I say the evil is here now! But there has always been and always will be evil. **What has changed today is the response I see from God's people**. God's people have sinned by ignoring this terrible scourge of our nation! We have chosen to walk on the other side of the street so we do not have to hear the screams of the innocents! We are walking with blinders so we don't have to see. Though we claim to be pro-life, we are angered with the protesters who carry the graphic signs of mutilated babies because it offends us, we would rather not know. To know makes us accountable to do something!

Above the door as you leave the last exhibit at the Holocaust Museum in Washington, D.C. is a plaque that reads:

First they came for the Socialists, and I did not speak out because I was not a Socialist. Then they came for the Trade Unionist and I did not speak out because I was not a Trade Unionist. Then they came for the Jews and I did not speak out because I was not a Jew. Then they came for me but there was no one left to speak for me.

Martin Neimoller (1892-1984) Lutheran minister and early Nazi supporter who was later imprisoned for opposing Hitler's regime

"All that is necessary for the triumph of evil is that good men do nothing" Edmund Burke

I believe it is not evil that brings the wrath of God upon a people. **I believe it is the apathy of God's people towards evil that brings the wrath of God upon a people.** Let me give you some thoughts from a very chilling story in Ezekiel Chapter 8 and 9. I would love to give you a study of the whole passage, but will have to just give you some portions of the story.

He said furthermore unto me, Son of man, seest thou what they do? even the great abominations that the house of Israel committeth here, that I should go far off from my sanctuary? but turn thee yet again, and thou shalt see greater abominations. (Ezekiel 8:6)

Then said he unto me, Son of man, hast thou seen what the ancients of the house of Israel do in the dark, every man in the chambers of his imagery? for they say, The LORD seeth us not; the LORD hath forsaken the earth. (Ezekiel 8:12)

Then he said unto me, Hast thou seen this, O son of man? Is it a light thing to the house of Judah that they commit the abominations which they commit here? for they have filled the land with violence, and have returned to provoke me to anger: and, lo, they put the branch to their nose. (Ezekiel 8:17)

We see that the Lord is very upset with Israel, but does this sound like America today? Do you suppose the Lord is upset with the murder of 56 million babies? Will God bring judgment upon us for this terrible scourge upon our nation? *Therefore will I also deal in fury: mine eye shall not spare, neither will I have pity: and though they cry in mine ears with a loud voice, yet will I not hear them. (Ezekiel 8:18)*

In Ezekiel Chapter 9 we see the judgment that God is going to bring upon His people.

He cried also in mine ears with a loud voice, saying, Cause them that have charge over the city to draw near, even every man with his <u>destroying weapon in his hand</u>. And, behold, six

177

men came from the way of the higher gate, which lieth toward the north, and every man a <u>slaughter weapon in his hand</u>; and one man among them was clothed with linen, with a writer's inkhorn by his side: and they went in, and stood beside the brasen altar. And the glory of the God of Israel was gone up from the cherub, whereupon he was, to the threshold of the house. And he called to the man clothed with linen, which had the writer's inkhorn by his side; And the LORD said unto him, **Go through the midst of the city, through the midst of Jerusalem, and set a mark upon the foreheads of the men that sigh and that cry for all the abominations that be done in the midst thereof.** *And to the others he said in mine hearing, Go ye after him through the city, and smite: let not your eye spare, neither have ye pity: <u>Slay utterly old and young, both maids, and little children, and women:</u> but come not near any man upon whom is the mark; and begin at my sanctuary. Then they began at the ancient men which were before the house. (Ezekiel 9:1-6)*

My friends, God is going to judge America for the slaughter of these innocent children. Abortion is a scourge upon our land and a reproach upon those who stand by and do nothing to stop it. That judgment may already be happening. What I want you to notice in this chilling passage is the attitude God has towards His people. God singles out the "Ancients" first, the older and wiser. They are held accountable first. But God ultimately holds all of society accountable as well for standing by while evil abounds. Notice however, that God tells the man with the inkhorn to put a mark on all those who sigh and weep over the sins of their nation. These people were spared the judgment of God. What I am trying to get you to see is that there are very few people even in our churches today who are weeping over the murder of the unborn. We are guilty of letting laws be changed. We allowed our leaders to legalize this terrible crime against nature. We have sat back and allowed these abortion clinics to be built in our cities. We have stopped weeping over this sin. In recent years we have even become experts at hiding ourselves from the stench of abortion. May we get our tears back before it is too late. I believe we are that final generation on earth right before the coming of the Lord.

(1 John 4:2-3) Hereby know ye the Spirit of God: Every spirit that confesseth that Jesus Christ is come in the flesh is of God: And every spirit that confesseth not that Jesus Christ is come in the flesh is not of God: and this is <u>that spirit of antichrist, whereof ye have heard that it should come; and even now already is it in the world.</u>

The spirit of Antichrist is already at work. This evil spirit of Antichrist will wax worse and worse until the trumpet sounds. Do you understand what I am saying? Can this nation and the world get much worse than it is now? Can the Church of Jesus Christ get any colder and apathetic than it is today? I believe the Antichrist is getting ready to come on the scene. America is far from being a Christian nation anymore. Friend, if you think it is bad now, just wait until the trumpet sounds and the saints are taken out of here. There is going to be an evil spread across this world to a degree that has never been seen or felt before. My point is, Scripture tells us that this will already be happening right before the Lord comes to take us home. I am saying it is here now! You had better have oil in your lamp!

5. Our Generation has witnessed the budding of the fig tree, the rebirth of the nation of Israel.

Did you know that Israel is the only nation in all of history that lost its statehood and then gained it back? For about 1900 years they were scattered all over the world with no homeland. From 70 AD to 1948/67. Actually, they had not been a sovereign nation since 605 B.C. when Babylon invaded their land. But in 70 A.D. they were chased from Israel and did not return until 1948. Most Bible scholars believe that the following Scripture is a reference to Israel.

(Matthew 24:32-34) Now learn a parable of the fig tree; When his branch is yet tender, and putteth forth leaves, ye know that summer is nigh: So likewise ye, when ye shall see all these things, know that it is near, even at the doors. Verily I say unto you, This generation shall not pass, till all these things be fulfilled.

As mentioned earlier concerning the Jubilee, the events in 1917 were the beginning of the return of the Jews to their homeland. You can do some research about the "Balfour" Agreements. The United Nations gave the land to them in May of 1948. But it is my belief that the *"budding of the fig tree"* was not complete until Israel got Jerusalem in the Six-Day War in 1967. It is our generation that has witnessed this. Many prophesy preachers of the past spoke of it. I am a fan of M.R. DeHaan. In his book "The Revelation" published in 1947, he said that one day Israel would be back in their land. He understood this from the word of God. His book came out just a year or so before it happened. DeHaan also said that one day man would break the sound barrier and even land men on the moon. We laugh at that now, but men like DeHaan, Larkin, and others were ahead of their time. They understood some things in their day that many missed. They understood some things about Israel before they returned to their homeland in 1948. Let me give you three things about Israel that need to be in place at the rapture.

1. Israel must be in their land.
2. Israel must be ready and in need of a peace treaty.
3. Israel must be ready for the temple.

You see, according to the following Scriptures, Israel must be in their land and ready for the peace treaty with Antichrist, and ready to resume the temple worship.

(2 Thessalonians 2:1-4) Now we beseech you, brethren, by the coming of our Lord Jesus Christ, and by our gathering together unto him, That ye be not soon shaken in mind, or be troubled, neither by spirit, nor by word, nor by letter as from us, as that the day of Christ is at hand. Let no man deceive you by any means: for that day shall not come, except there come a falling away first, and that man of sin be revealed, the son of perdition; Who opposeth and exalteth himself above all that is called God, or that is worshipped; so that he as God sitteth in the temple of God, shewing himself that he is God.

(Daniel 9:27) And he shall confirm the covenant with many for one week: and in the midst of the week he shall cause the sacrifice and the oblation to cease, and for the overspreading of abominations he shall make it desolate, even until the consummation, and that determined shall be poured upon the desolate.

(Revelation 6:1-2) And I saw when the Lamb opened one of the seals, and I heard, as it were the noise of thunder, one of the four beasts saying, Come and see. And I saw, and behold a white horse: and he that sat on him had a bow; and a crown was given unto him: and he went forth conquering, and to conquer.

Brethren, this has all taken place in our generation. Men of the prior generation saw it and wrote about it, but it was fulfilled in our generation. Israel is in their land. They are in desperate need of peace. They will resume the temple worship either right before or right after the Antichrist comes on the scene.

Look up fellow Christian, our *redemption draweth nigh.* Jesus is coming soon. We fit the description of that last and final generation upon the earth when Messiah comes for us. The spiritual and moral conditions are here. The one-world financial and judicial system is here. The political beast is here. The Laodicean Church is all around us. The whole world "*groaneth in travail*" awaiting the redemption that is to come.

He which testifieth these things saith, Surely I come quickly. Amen. Even so, come, Lord Jesus. Revelation 22:20

2520

Chapter 16

A strange title for a chapter, but when you understand what it means you will not ever forget it. Several years ago while studying prophecy I discovered that Daniel's 70th week (the seven-year Tribulation Period) is not actually measured in years but in months and days. After more research, I found that apart from Daniel Chapter 9 calling them weeks of years, the Tribulation is always referred to in months or in days. You see, our calendar is based on the sun while the Jewish calendar is based on the moon. Our year is 365 ¼ days while Israel has a 354 2/3rd day year. God's prophetic calendar is based on a perfect 360 day year.

When God gives the length of the Tribulation, he gives it in two segments of time. The first half is 42 months and the second half is 42 months. You might be thinking that is 3 ½ years and I am not denying that but that is not exactly accurate. You see, 3 ½ years on our calendar is 42 months, but it is not the same as 42 months on God's calendar. Forty-two months on God's timeline is exactly 1,260 days. In fact several times God measures the two halves of the Tribulation as 1,260 day periods of time. Look at these verses of Scripture that give the duration in months and years:

Revelation 11:2 But the court which is without the temple leave out, and measure it not; for it is given unto the Gentiles: and the holy city shall they tread under foot forty and two months.

Revelation 11:3 And I will give power unto my two

witnesses, and they shall prophesy a thousand two hundred and threescore days, clothed in sackcloth.

Revelation 12:6 And the woman fled into the wilderness, where she hath a place prepared of God, that they should feed her there a thousand two hundred and threescore days.

Revelation13:5 And there was given unto him a mouth speaking great things and blasphemies; and power was given unto him to continue forty and two months.

(Daniel 7:25) And he shall speak great words against the most High, and shall wear out the saints of the most High, and think to change times and laws: and they shall be given into his hand until a time and times and the dividing of time.

(Revelation 12:14) And to the woman were given two wings of a great eagle, that she might fly into the wilderness, into her place, where she is nourished for a time, and times, and half a time, from the face of the serpent.

All these passages are dealing with the timeline of the 70ᵗʰ week. They all break it up into two halves of 1,260 days which is 42 months. (Also called time, times and a half) God is being very specific with the number of days and months. Because of this, I believe we too must be specific. The Tribulation is two periods of 1,260 days each (42 month halves) which make up the complete 70ᵗʰ week of Daniel Chapter 9. Therefore the Tribulation is 2,520 days long. I believe there is a principle taught here that is very important. The principle is that God measures time as 360 day years, not 365 ¼ as we do. We dealt with this in another chapter so I will not spend much time on it here. If we are going to understand timelines and figure out where we are in history, we need to use the same standard for measuring as the Lord uses. It is plain in the following Scriptures that God does expect us to keep up with times and seasons as well as be aware that we are in the last days upon this earth.

(Genesis 1:14) And God said, Let there be lights in the firmament of the heaven to divide the day from the night; and let them be for signs, and for seasons, and for days, and years:

(Psalms 90:12) So teach us to number our days, that we may apply our hearts unto wisdom.

(2 Timothy 3:1) This know also, that in the last days perilous times shall come.

Several things have hindered this generation from understanding where we are on God's prophetic timeline.
1. The false notion that the New Testament began at the birth of Christ rather than at Calvary. We discussed this already, but be sure you understand that The Old Testament Age ended at the renting of the veil with the death of the Testator, the Lord Jesus Christ. (See chapter 14)
2. The Gregorian Calendar of 365 ¼ day years has also thrown us off track. By the way, both of these falsehoods came from the teaching of Rome and were passed on to us through the Protestants. God uses a 360 day year when He measures time. If we are going to understand where we are on the prophetic clock, we too need to use this 360 day year. There are **36.75 extra days** in a seven year period on our solar calendar.
3. A moving away from figurative and prophetic interpretation of the Scriptures. (See chapter 4)

These three things have caused much confusion and uncertainty about the timeline of last day events and the understanding of where we are in the history of the world. It is my belief that we are very near the end of the 2000th year of the Church Age.

185

2520 days yet to come

There are 2,520 days left of the 70 weeks of Daniel that have not yet been fulfilled. Remember, Daniel 9:24-27 teaches us that there are 70 weeks of years determined upon Israel. These weeks equal 490 years total. There is one week left to be fulfilled which is seven years long and made up of exactly 2,520 days . **The entire Church Age of 2000 years (two days of creative week) has been placed in between the time Messiah is "*cut off*" and the time the saints are "*caught up*."** I believe it is possible that Calvary ended on the year 3993 and that the final 2,520 days of the Tribulation finish off that final seven years of the Old Testament. Nobody can be sure when the 2000 years will be complete. The calendar has been messed with. We do not know the exact year of Calvary to even begin the count. We can guess, but the Bible says "*No man knows the day or hour*" of the coming of the Lord. I believe we are very close. That is the reason for the writing of this book.

There are some interesting things about 2,520 in the Bible that I wish to share with you. As I said, there are two equal halves of the Tribulation. They are each 1,260 days long. I believe that Feast of Passover is right in the middle of these two periods. I believe it is the Antichrist entering the Temple on Passover that separates the two parts. Let me give you some interesting things about 2,520 that I believe you will find quite eye opening.

1. The Tribulation Period is 2,520 days long.
2. There are 2,520 days from a new moon (Feast of Trumpets) in the fall to the Day of Atonement seven years later.

As we discussed earlier, Day of Atonement is the sixth Feast. It is the day that is prophetic of Christ returning to the earth with the Title Deed in His hand to reclaim what is His.

186

I believe it will happen on a Jubilee year. I decided to try something that I do not know if anyone has ever done. After all, very few people today know anything about the seven feasts and even fewer understand the beginning of the New Testament at Calvary. Since the Day of Atonement represents the day that Christ returns at the end of the Tribulation, I went into the future a few years and found the Day of Atonement on the Jewish Calendar. I have a program on my computer that will give the exact number of days between any two dates you program into it. What I found shocked me. I found that there are 2,520 days from Day of Atonement back to a new moon in either October or November. Remember, the Feast of Trumpets is on the new moon in the fall in the Jewish month of Tishri. That is September or October on our calendar. What I have just shared with you is not in any book anywhere that I know of, nor have I ever heard it mentioned anywhere. I analyzed eight years in a row from 2008-2015. Below is a chart of the eight years I researched and what I found:

New Moon in the Fall	Total Days	Day of Atonement (Yom Kippur)
10/282008	2520	09/23/2015
11/16/2009	2520	10/12/2016
11/06/2010	2520	09/30/2017
10/26/2011	2520	09/19/2018
11/13/2012	2520	10/09/2019
11/03/2013	2520	09/28/2020
10/23/2014	2520	09/16/2021
11/11/2015	2520	10/05/2022

What does it mean? Well, it simply proves that God is a God of order and that things are going to happen exactly as He says they will happen. And it is further proof that God is serious about the 2,520 days. Numbers and dates and the timing of events are all important to God. When the rapture occurs, whenever it happens will be the perfect day. God's calendar is perfect. God operates on His own Biblical calendar. We will never grasp these things using our corrupt system of counting days. You see, if you try to get seven exact years from Feast of Trumpets on the Jewish calendar to the Day of Atonement on our solar calendar, it never comes out right. This has baffled me for years. In seven years time there are 36.75 more days on our Gregorian calendar than there are on God's 360 day prophetic calendar. When you use a 360 day calendar it comes out perfectly to the new moon in October or November every time! Now the Feast of Trumpets is not in the month of November. It is always in September or October on our calendar. What does this mean? It means this: "NO MAN KNOWS THE DAY OR HOUR." That is not what we want to hear but it is the truth. It may also mean that the Feast of Trumpets on the Jewish calendar is NOT the Feast of Trumpets on God's prophetic calendar. Personally, I think the Lord will come for us in the fall of the year because that is harvest time and the rapture is the harvest of souls. I also think He will come on a new moon. But nobody can be sure about these things. We have no way to be sure the Day of Atonement is right on the Jewish calendar the Jews use today. See, nobody can be sure of anything. If the trumpet were to sound on a new moon in October or November, that would give an exact 2,520 days until the Day of Atonement in the seventh solar year. But you will never be able to figure days and months unless you use the standard Biblical 360 day year that God uses. It would be like going to the store to buy carpet to do a 9X12 room and the clerk uses a 32" yard stick to measure with. You are not going to have enough to cover your floor. Now before anyone starts setting dates, the Lord could come on the new moon in any fall month and that would be the Feast of Trumpets. 2,520 days later would be the Day of

Atonement even though it is not the date marked on the Jewish calendar we use. Do you see what I am saying? Be careful about trying to figure out the exact day, month, or year. You will never be able to be sure about this. The Lord could come back in the summer and that could be His Feast of Trumpets! I often tell folks that I am a season setter not a date setter. I strongly believe the Lord expects us to "see the day approaching" but not "know the day or hour." Please do not think I am saying the Lord is coming on a new moon in October or November. What I do know is that His return is very soon. I believe the rapture is a fulfillment of Feast of Trumpets. I suspect the Lord will come for us in the fall of the year, but I can not be sure.

3. There are approximately 2,520 years from the captivity in Babylon to 1948 when Israel became a nation.

It is very interesting to me that there are approximately 2,520 years from the Babylonian captivity where Israel lost it's statehood until 1948 where they regained it again. You have to ignore Ussher's dates because he started the New Testament at the birth of Christ with 4 B.C. 1948 is the date Israel got back in their land. If you subtract the life of Christ it becomes 1915. Add 605 to that and you get 2,520. I realize they rebuilt the temple and the walls in the books of Ezra and Nehemiah, but they were never fully out from under the control of heathen nations. Even when Jesus came on the scene, they were under Roman rule. In 70 A.D. the last temple was destroyed by the Romans. My point is that after 2,520 years Israel became a sovereign state. Is that not amazing in light of the fact that the Tribulation is 2,520 days? If you are not familiar with the 70 year Babylonian captivity, you need to do some serious study on it. There is so much of the Bible that revolves around this time period. The entire books of Ezekiel and Jeremiah take place just before Nebuchadnezzar takes Jerusalem. The attack occurred in two stages and the date of this attack is approximately 605-586 B.C. The book of Daniel starts off in Chapter 1 with a young Hebrew lad named Daniel being taken into captivity. The last half of the book of Daniel as well as Ezra, Nehemiah, and Esther are all post captivity books. When you begin to understand these time periods, the Bible will begin to make so much more sense to you. 1948 is when Israel became a nation again. It had been approximately 2,520 years since they lost their statehood in the Babylonian captivity. The captivity which lasted 70 years ended when the nation of Persia defeated Babylon and became the world power under Cyrus. The Jews were given freedoms and allowed to rebuild the city, but they were never actually out from under the dictatorship of these world empires. From 70 A.D. to 1948 they were scattered and persecuted all over the world. Do you think getting statehood after 2,520 years after the Babylonian captivity is significant?

4. There are approximately 2,520 years from Feast of Purim to 2017.

Things are about to get even more interesting. Not only is it 2,520 years from the Babylonian captivity to the re-gathering of the Jewish people into a nation again in May of 1948, but there is more. There are approximately 2,520 years from the Feast of Purim to the end of the year 2017. Do not confuse the Feast of Purim with the seven feasts. The Feast of Purim is not at all related to the Seven Feasts of the Lord. Feast of Purim was started in the book of Esther. The book of Esther takes place right at the end of the 70 year Babylonian captivity when the Medes and the Persians fought against Babylon and defeated them. Somewhere along here is the story of Esther who becomes the queen in the place of Vashti. As you recall, wicked Haman devised a plan to kill all the Jews on the 13th of the month Adar. Esther exposes this evil plan to the king and Haman is hanged on the gallows he had built for Mordecai. The king passes a law giving the Jews permission to defend themselves, and on Adar 13 they win a great victory. The Jews made it a national feast day. Every year since then they have celebrated the Feast of Purim. The month Adar is usually in December on our calendar. This event was approximately 70 years after the Babylonian captivity took place in Daniel Chapter 1. That means it is approximately 2,520 years from Feast of Purim to 2017 or 2018. The Feast of Purim dates to approximately 520 B.C. Add that to the 2000 years of the New Testament and you get 2,520 years. What does all this mean? It means once again that God is a God of order. Every event and number in the Bible is on purpose and has significant figurative meaning. Again, our calendar is wrong and so is the Jewish calendar. We can not be sure of the years of the Babylonian captivity. There are in fact several different dates claimed as the date anywhere from 605 to 586 B.C. So once again, there is no way to know for sure where that 2,520th year is. Just know that it is close. The 1948 date with Israel becoming a nation is an interesting possibility for that 2,520th year though wouldn't you agree?

5. **The Tribulation is exactly 2,520 days but not necessarily 7 solar years in length.**

It hit me suddenly a few years back while thinking on these things. Why does God make such a big deal of specifying two periods of exact 1,260 days which are 42 months each? I think because it is the fulfillment of Daniel's 70th week that it is required to be exactly 2,520 days total. Secondly, I think God is making clear that it is days not years because it in fact may not be seven years at all! Now stay with me here. Let me give you some Scriptures to look at

191

that I think will shed some light.

(Genesis 1:5) And God called the light Day, and the darkness he called Night. And the <u>evening and the morning were the first day</u>.

A day in the Bible starts in the evening at sundown. A day is an evening and a morning. It does not say how many hours are in a day. We know there are 24 hours, but God does not specify that there <u>has</u> to be 24 hours in a day. God says a day is an evening and a morning. This is important so don't miss it. We have become so set in our customs and beliefs that we often miss the simple truths of the Bible. Look at Genesis Chapter 1 again. Look at each of the seven days that are mentioned. Not one time does God ever say that a day has to have 24 hours in it. A day is an evening and a morning and that is that. In the following verses, notice that Jesus is speaking of the Tribulation.

(Matthew 24:21-22) For then shall be great tribulation, such as was not since the beginning of the world to this time, no, nor ever shall be. And <u>except those days should be shortened,</u> there should no flesh be saved: but for the elect's sake those <u>days shall be shortened</u>.

It is going to be a terrible time of sorrow and suffering. Jesus says that unless the days should be shortened, no flesh would be saved from the destruction. I had some discussion with a friend about this a few years back. My friend thought that maybe God was going to shorten the Tribulation in order to save the world from destroying itself. That is a good assumption except for the fact that God said the Tribulation would be exactly 2,520 days long. Two periods of 1,260 days each. **I believe this passage could be saying that God is going to speed up the days.** In other words, God could be going to make the evening and morning go by faster. God would simply speed up the spin of the earth and a day would go by faster. The moon would maintain its exact relation to the earth no matter how fast the earth spins. It would travel across the sky at the same relative speed as the earth spins. I think it is very probable that God is going to speed up the spin of the earth during the Tribulation. I believe that is what these passages could be teaching us.

(Revelation 8:12)   And the fourth angel sounded, and the <u>third</u> part of the sun was smitten, and the <u>third</u> part of the moon, and the <u>third</u> part of the stars; so as the <u>third part of them was darkened, and the day shone not for a third part of it, and the night likewise.</u>

I believe the 2,520 days could go by at a much faster pace than they do now. In other words, there is a certain point in the solar system where the earth will be in its travel around the sun at the end of the 6000th year. It could be that the days are going to happen at a rate that will allow the 2,520 days to take place in a much shorter solar time period. Revelation 8:12 seems to be saying the night and the day will be 1/3rd shorter. If the earth spins faster by 1/3 there would be a third less sun and a third less moon and stars each day. God has changed the rotation speed of the earth before. In fact, God made time go backwards.

(2 Kings 20:8-11) And Hezekiah said unto Isaiah, What shall be the sign that the LORD will heal me, and that I shall go up into the house of the LORD the third day? And Isaiah said, This sign shalt thou have of the LORD, that the LORD will do the thing that he hath spoken: shall the shadow go forward ten degrees, or go back ten degrees? And Hezekiah answered, It is a light thing for the shadow to go down ten degrees: nay, but let the shadow return backward ten degrees. And Isaiah the prophet cried unto the LORD: and he brought the shadow ten degrees backward, by which it had gone down in the dial of Ahaz.

Look at what God did here for Joshua:

(Joshua 10:13) And the sun stood still, and the moon stayed, until the people had avenged themselves upon their enemies. Is not this written in the book of Jasher? So the sun stood still in the midst of heaven, and hasted not to go down about a whole day.

What I am trying to get you to see is that the Tribulation is 2,520 days long. Those days are very possibly going to go by faster than they do now. It is very possible that the 2,520 days could go by in just 3-4 years as we understand time today. In other words, the Tribulation could squeeze all the necessary days needed into a much shorter time on the solar clock.

6. Some interesting 2,520 numerology.

The following are some very interesting variables of the number 2,520 using God's prophetic 360 day calendar.

-7000 years is equal to 2,520,000 days.
-2,520,000 days is equal to 360,000 weeks.
-70 years is equal to 25,200 days.
-25,200 days equals 3600 weeks.
-7 years is equal to 2,520 days.
-2,520 days is equal to 360 weeks.
-2,520 years is equal to 360 weeks of years (7 year weeks).

7000 years is the whole history of the earth.
70 years is the length of the Babylonian Captivity.
Seven years is the length of the Tribulation and the definition of a Biblical week. Seven is God's Sabbath. It is the number of completion and perfection. 360 is God's prophetic year and is the variable within all the "weeks" in these statistics.

194

SIGNS IN THE HEAVENS
Chapter 17

Several years ago I learned about the coming blood red moons in Israel. Prophesy preachers have been talking about them in recent months and there are some books on the subject that have only recently been published. You have to be very careful about what you find on the internet and even what you find at the Christian Book store. There is some bad information coming from both sides concerning the topic of the blood red moons. In this chapter I am going to give you a brief explanation of the blood red moons and how they appear to line up prophetically. I want to make it very clear that I am not predicting the rapture or the second coming. I am simply going to make you aware of something very interesting happening in the heavens. I am going to ignore some of the hype you may have read on the internet and just give you the facts as I see them.

There are four consecutive total lunar eclipses coming in Israel in 2014 and 2015. These lunar eclipses, or blood red moons as they are called, are on Biblical Feast days. I should not have to tell you how significant that is. I will explain it all as we go but first we need to understand that the sun, the moon, and the stars have a purpose for their being. They are there to give us heat and light, and thank goodness for that. They are also there to measure days and months and years. However, they are also there for signs. Look what the Bible says:

(Psalms 19:1-3) The heavens declare the glory of God; and the firmament sheweth his handywork. Day unto day uttereth speech, and night unto night sheweth knowledge. There is no speech nor language, where their voice is not heard.

Notice that the heavens speak to all regardless of tongue,

language or nationality. This could go hand in hand with this passage of Scripture: *There was a man sent from God, whose name was John. The same came for a witness, to bear witness of the Light, that all men through him might believe. He was not that Light, but was sent to bear witness of that Light. That was <u>the true Light, which lighteth every man that cometh into the world</u>. (John 1:6-9)*

(Genesis 1:14) And God said, Let there be lights in the firmament of the heaven to divide the day from the night; and let them be for signs, and for seasons, and for days, and years:

These *"lights"* are the sun, the moon, and the stars. They are for giving light and for dividing night from day. They are also for signs and seasons.

(Joel 2:30-31) And I will shew <u>wonders</u> in the heavens and in the earth, blood, and fire, and pillars of smoke. The sun shall be turned into darkness, and the <u>moon into blood</u>, before the great and the terrible day of the LORD come.

(Acts 2:19-20) And I will shew wonders in heaven above, and <u>signs</u> in the earth beneath; blood, and fire, and vapour of smoke: The sun shall be turned into darkness, and the moon into blood, before that great and notable day of the Lord come:
(Luke 21:25) And there shall be <u>signs in the sun, and in the moon</u>, and in the stars; and upon the earth distress of nations, with perplexity; the sea and the waves roaring;

Let me explain these lunar eclipses or, blood red moons as they are called.
1. A blood red moon is a total lunar eclipse.
A partial lunar eclipse is never called a blood red moon.

Only a total lunar eclipse is considered a blood red moon. It is caused when the earth gets between the sun and the moon. The moon appears "red" because of the rays of the sun going through the earth's atmosphere.

2. A "tetrad" is four consecutive TOTAL lunar eclipses in a row.

There have been many blood red moons (total lunar eclipses) throughout history. There is nothing at all unusual about a lunar eclipse occurring. There have also been several tetrads throughout history. Though not real common, it is nothing all that unusual either. Let me be sure you understand, a tetrad is four TOTAL lunar eclipses in a row. Three total lunar eclipses and one partial lunar eclipse would not be considered a tetrad in the scientific community.

3. An extremely rare tetrad is taking place in 2014/2015.

Remember, a "tetrad" is a scientific term that simply means four total lunar eclipses in a row. What is rare in 2014/2015 is the fact that these four lunar eclipses are going to occur on feast days in Israel. They are going to happen on Feast of Passover and Feast of Tabernacles in 2014 and the same two feasts in 2015. Two years in a row there will be a full lunar eclipse on these two same feast days. Now, this has my attention! Is it getting your attention?

4. There are some interesting and prophetic lessons about the occurrence of blood moons on Jewish Feast days.

Passover is the first and Tabernacles is the last of the Seven Feasts of the Lord. It is also interesting that the seven feasts all take place in a space of seven months. (Nisan - Tishri) If I don't have you on the edge of your seat now, you are just not thinking! Seven is God's number of completion. There are seven churches in Revelation, seven trumpets, seven angels, seven seals, seven vials. We could go on and on with the "sevens" in the Bible. There are seven days of

197

creation. I believe there will be seven thousand years of human history. The Tribulation is seven years. There are seven days in a week. Now we learn that there is a blood red moon on the 1st and 7th of the seven feasts that take place in the first seven months of the Jewish calendar? Yes, this has got my attention! But wait, there is more…much more.

5. There have been seven tetrads in the whole 2000 year New Testament Age where the blood red moons fell on the Jewish feasts of Passover and Tabernacles.

Seven times in the last 2000 years there has been a rare occurrence of these four back-to-back full lunar blood red moons on the feasts of Passover and Tabernacles. Have I still got your attention? I have checked this out on the NASA website myself. I am not telling you something I have not verified. It is amazing when I scour you-tube as well as articles on the web at how many mistakes there are in what people are saying. One guy makes an honest typo or mistake and fifty other people copy that mistake until it all becomes a big mess.

*** The NASA website is: http://eclipse.gsfc.nasa.gov/eclipse.html

6. There is an eighth tetrad coming in 2014 and 2015.

Make sure you understand what I am telling you. Seven times in the entire New Testament Age there has been a tetrad on these same two feast days. Each occurrence was on Passover and Tabernacles two consecutive years in a row. In the last 2000 years this has only happened seven times. There is an eighth occurrence coming in 2014/2015.

Pastor Mark Biltz is the first person I heard talking about these blood red moons back in 2008. He went to the NASA website and found all the lunar eclipses and tetrads throughout history. What he found was shocking. Mark Biltz said the following as quoted in a newsletter from 2008 by J.R. Church:

"He focused on the precise times of solar and lunar eclipses, sometimes called "blood moons," by logging onto NASA's website on eclipses. He noticed a rare phenomenon of four consecutive total lunar eclipses which are known as a "tetrad." During this century, tetrads occur at least six times, but the only string of four consecutive "blood moons" coincide with God's Holy days of Passover and the Feast of Tabernacles. This occurs between the years 2014 and 2015 on today's Gregorian calendar.

In the 20th century, he noticed that such successive blood moons coinciding with Passover and Tabernacles occurred only on 1967-68, the year the Jews liberated Jerusalem from the control of the Arabs. He also noted that the only other such combination of eclipses in the 20th century took place in 1949-50, the year following the Jewish state's hard-fought war of independence, when Israel became a nation.

7. Each of the first seven tetrads are associated with an important historical event that corresponded to Israel.

Since the seven tetrads all revolved around Israel, it is very possible that the eighth will too. In fact, I would say it is more than possible, I would say it is almost a certainty. Let's look at the tetrads throughout history that fell on Jewish feast days and see what we can learn. There will no doubt be some prophetic lessons for us.

Here are the dates of all eight tetrads that occur from Calvary to the end of the 21st century:

1. 162/163 A.D.
2. 795/796 A.D.
3. 842/843 A.D.
4. 860/861 A.D.

There were some historical events for Israel during these first four tetrad years but we will not take the time to discuss them. They are certainly not as significant as the ones to follow so I will not take the time on them. However, I assure you there is a connection to Israel in these first four. The next four times are quite significant and I want us to look at them.

5. 1493/1494 A.D.

In 1492 Columbus left Spain to discover the new world. He is credited with finding America which God raised up for two purposes. First, America would be used to spread the gospel around the world. Second, God would use America to protect and be a future haven for the Jews. In 1493 King Ferdinand and Queen Isabella of Spain ordered all Jewish people to leave the country. They were given 14 days to get out and could only take what they could carry. (The Spanish Inquisition also was begun a few years prior and continued on for many years.) A few months after the Jews were expelled from Spain, the series of blood red moons began in Israel. All total lunar eclipses and all on Passover and Tabernacles for two consecutive years.

6. 1949/1950 A.D.

Israel returned to the land of Israel in May of 1948. However, they fought a war for several months with the surrounding Arab nations before they officially seated their new government. They also got a seat on the United Nations in January of 1949. Passover was four months later and began the series of four blood red moons. Again, all four were full lunar eclipses and all on the Feast of Passover and Tabernacles for two consecutive years.

7. 1967/1968 A.D.

In June of 1967, Israel was attacked once again. It was a miraculous victory for the Jews that resulted in the acquiring of Gaza and the Golan Heights as well as Jerusalem. It is called the Six-Day War. On Passover in April of 1967 began the first of four blood red moons. All four were full lunar eclipses and all four fell on the same two feasts of Passover and Tabernacles. This tetrad began two months before the Six-Day War.

8. 2014/2015 A.D.

An eighth tetrad is occurring in the near future and on those same feast days. There will be a blood red moon on Feast of Passover April 15th in 2014. Then on Tabernacles the same year. The same on Passover and Tabernacles in 2015. There are no more of these "tetrads" on Jewish feast days for the rest of this century. By the way, there are also two solar eclipses coming in Israel with the first on March 20th, 2015. That is the 1st of Nisan which is 14 days before Passover. The second solar eclipse is seven months later on September 13th which is Feast of Trumpets. Is it interesting that the two solar eclipses are on the same first and last of the seven months? In 2014/2015 we not only have the four blood red moons on Jewish feast days, but we have two solar eclipses and one of them is on a feast day! So what does all this mean? In the Bible the moon seems to be a sign for the nation of Israel. **There have only been seven Blood Moon Tetrads on these feast days between Jesus Christ's first coming and 2013**. Remember, we are talking about total lunar eclipses on the feasts of Passover and Tabernacles two consecutive years in a row making them a very rare event that scientists call a tetrad. Each and every time there was some significant event which impacted the Jewish people. All seven times that it has happened in the last 2000 years something happened concerning the Jews. Seven times this rare occurrence fell on the first and last of the seven feasts that are in a seven month period on the Jewish calendar and we have preachers around the country scoffing at it? Can you believe that?

Seven is God's number of completion. The 8th occurrence of a tetrad begins on Passover on April 15th 2014. Then a blood red moon on Feast of Tabernacles October the 8th and the same occurrence on the same two feasts in 2015. Eight is the number of man. It is also the number of new beginnings. When the whole earth was covered with the flood, Noah "the eighth person" (2 Peter 2:5) stepped out of the ark to commence a new order of things. "Eight souls" (1 Peter 3:20) were saved from the flood and replenished the earth. It was a new beginning. I am not saying the rapture is coming on one of these blood red moons nor can we be sure any of this has anything at all to do with the end-times. I am saying it will most likely have something to do with Israel. Something may take place concerning Israel either before or shortly after the blood red moons. Now, the rapture would certainly be a big event for Israel because it sets up the rise of Antichrist and the seven-year peace treaty with them. Again, I am not saying that is what is coming. I am saying that something always happened concerning Israel at the time of these four blood red moons in history. I believe there will be something big this time as well.

Here are the dates of the blood red moons and solar eclipses as they occur in 2014-2015.

* Passover - April 15, 2014
* Tabernacles - Oct. 8, 2014
* Passover - April 4, 2015
* Tabernacles - Sept. 28, 2015

Two solar eclipses:
* March 20, 2015 (14 days before Passover, 1st of Nisan)
* September 13, 2015 (Eve of Feast of Trumpets 29th of Elul)

9-11, The Stock Market, and Prophecy

September 11, 2001, was a huge historical event. Probably bigger than any of us realize. About 3000 were killed that day. I have some questions about it all that will never be answered this side of Heaven, but that is for another book. Is there a connection between 9-11 and the coming tetrad and solar eclipses? As a matter of fact there may be. I read an article on World Net Daily concerning this very subject. The story was an interview with Jonathan Cahn who authored a book called, THE HARBINGER. Cahn mentions three events that all happen on the 29th of Elul on the Jewish calendar. That date just happens to be the evening before

Feast of Trumpets, the 1st of Tishri. It is usually September on our calendar. Below are the three events.

1. 9-17-2001 (29th of Elul) the stock market lost near 700 points six days after the twin towers fell.
2. 9-29-2008 (29th of Elul) the stock market fell 777.7 points and closed down 7% in all.
3. 9-13-15 (29th of Elul) is the evening of Rosh Hashanah (Feast of Trumpets) in Israel. It is also a solar eclipse.

All three of these dates are the exact same day on the Jewish Calendar, the 29th of Elul, which is the eve before day one of the month Tishri. The 1st of Tishri is not only Feast of Trumpets, but it is also the start of the new year in Israel. Jews call it Rosh Hashanah which means "head of the year." To them it is like our January 1st. It is their beginning of the next year on the secular calendar. They also believe God created the world on the 1st of Tishri.

After reading this story I began to think about it in light of the many truths I have shared in this book. I began to look for some prophetic pictures and types. First thing I noticed was the seven year periods of time between each event, exactly right to the day. I also noticed that the stock market losses were almost identical and the 777.7 is just stunning. I actually remember when it happened. I was preaching a prophecy conference in St. Louis, Missouri, on September 28-30, 2008. I was with my friend, Pastor Bill Waugh, and we were almost sure the Lord was coming the next day which was Trumpets! Another thing I see is that each of these three dates falls on what the Jews believe is a Sabbatical year. Do you remember we talked about that a few chapters back? After the end of the sixth year the Jews would let the land rest for the seventh year. It was a Sabbath for the land. The Jews believe the next Sabbatical year begins the 1ˢᵗ of Tishri of 2014 and ends on the 1ˢᵗ of Tishri 2015. I do not know if they are right, but it is interesting. If they are right, then each of these three events happened on Sabbatical years, or perhaps I should say they happened right at the end of the Sabbatical year. Then you begin to think about the tetrad of the four blood red moons in 2014/2015 and the solar eclipse on 3/20/15 which is the 1ˢᵗ of Nisan on the Jews calendar. That is the beginning of their religious year. Then we have the solar eclipse seven months later on the eve of their secular year at the very last day of the Sabbatical year. Does this sound interesting to you? I do not know anything for sure, I am just saying that everything we have talked about in this book is pointing towards the soon return of the Lord.

*The sun shall be turned into darkness, and the moon into blood, **before** the great and the terrible day of the LORD come.*
Joel 2:31

WHAT IN THE WORLD IS GOING ON?
Chapter 18

Mark 13:8 For nation shall rise against nation, and kingdom against kingdom: and there shall be earthquakes in divers places, and there shall be famines and troubles: these are the beginnings of sorrows.

Isaiah 24:20 The earth shall reel to and fro like a drunkard, and shall be removed like a cottage; and the transgression thereof shall be heavy upon it; and it shall fall, and not rise again.

Luke 21:11 And great earthquakes shall be in divers places, and famines, and pestilences; and fearful sights and great signs shall there be from heaven.

Luke 21:25-26 And there shall be signs in the sun, and in the moon, and in the stars; and upon the earth distress of nations, with perplexity; the sea and the waves roaring; Men's hearts failing them for fear, and for looking after those things which are coming on the earth: for the powers of heaven shall be shaken.

These Scriptures could almost be out of today's newspapers. It seems like every week there is another shocking story. You can not even keep up with all the strange things happening around the world. As you hear more and more tragedies unfold around the globe, do you ever find yourself asking, **"What in the world is going on?"**

Consider these events from just the month of February 2013:

FEB 14: 6.9 earthquake reported in Russia.
FEB 15 : Meteorites hit Russia at 9:23 AM causing panic in three cities.
FEB 15: Asteroid DA-14 comes within 17,000 miles of earth, closer than some satellites.
FEB 15: 7:44 PM a meteor streaks across San Francisco skies.
FEB 16: A 6.2 earthquake in the Philippians.
FEB 16: A 6.0 earthquake in New Zealand.
FEB 16: A meteor streaks across the skies of Miami, Fl.
FEB 20: Huge Midwest snowstorm hits the USA.
FEB 21: Big seas reported in Gold Coast, Florida.
FEB 21: Sicily and Athens, Greece, report violent thunder storms and floods with 50 liters in just a half hour and cars swept away.
FEB 21: Sink holes on highway in Page, Arizona .
FEB 21: Wales, Australia reports flooding and severe weather.
FEB 24: Sydney, Australia reports savage storms.
FEB 27: West Australia clocks a Cyclone at 250 km/h. (150 mph)

These are just some of the bizarre events that made the news in February of 2013. **"What in the world is going on?"** Could it be that we are in the last days and God is preparing the world for something? It is plainly taught in the Bible that God often uses nature to carry out His will. Look at the following Scriptures:

Matthew 27:54 Now when the centurion, and they that were with him, watching Jesus, saw the <u>earthquake</u>, and those things that were done, they feared greatly, saying, Truly this was the Son of God.

Matthew 28:2 And, behold, there was <u>a great earthquake</u>: for the angel of the Lord descended from heaven, and came and rolled back the stone from the door, and sat upon it.

Acts 16:26 And suddenly there was <u>a great earthquake</u>, so that the foundations of the prison were shaken: and immediately all the doors were opened, and every one's bands were loosed.

Revelation 6:12 And I beheld when he had opened the sixth

seal, and, lo, there was a great earthquake; and the sun became black as sackcloth of hair, and the moon became as blood;

Revelation 8:5 And the angel took the censer, and filled it with fire of the altar, and cast it into the earth: and there were voices, and thunderings, and lightnings, and an earthquake.

Revelation 11:13 And the same hour was there a great earthquake, and the tenth part of the city fell, and in the earthquake were slain of men seven thousand: and the remnant were affrighted, and gave glory to the God of heaven.

Revelation 11:19 And the temple of God was opened in heaven, and there was seen in his temple the ark of his testament: and there were lightnings, and voices, and thunderings, and an earthquake, and great hail.

Revelation 16:18 And there were voices, and thunders, and lightnings; and there was a great earthquake, such as was not since men were upon the earth, so mighty an earthquake, and so great.

Now let's take a look at what is happening right here in America, in "the land of the free and the home of the brave." As you read through this list I want you to realize that some of these things were considered just "Conspiracy Theories" a few short years ago. These can no longer be ignored or scoffed at; the following list is absolute fact.

- FEMA camps now exist in every state.
- Government listening in on citizens phone calls.
  (Even spying on Congress)
- Citizens can be arrested and held without a warrant.
- American citizens can and have been killed by drones over seas without a trial.

- Senator Rand Paul held up the Senate for 13 hours awaiting a statement from the Obama administration stating they have no authority to kill citizens in the USA without a trial.

- DHS has ordered over 1.6 billion rounds of hollow point ammo. That is enough to shoot every American citizen five times. Experts tell us hollow points are more expensive and are NOT for target practice.

- War games/training between military and police in several cities across the country including Los Angeles, Houston, Miami and others.

- Record number of Americans on food stamps and other "entitlements."

- Homeland Security has ordered 750 armored trucks for domestic use.

- Chief Justice Roberts of the Supreme Court determined Obamacare to be a tax and that the Federal Government can now force citizens to buy a product or service they do not want.

- The legalization of gay marriage across our land.

- Leaders in Government who are surrounded by armed guards and who often carry concealed weapons themselves, while demanding that citizens be disarmed.

Friend, this is just the tip of the iceberg. This is right out of Hitler's Germany. The problem is that most Americans do not think it can happen here. Well, I want to tell you that not only CAN it happen but that it IS happening. Are you asking yourself the following question yet: **"What in the world is going on?"** The Bible says, *But evil men and seducers shall wax worse and worse, deceiving, and being deceived. (2Timothy 3:13)*

I am going to give you three things that I believe are going on in the world, but first let me throw one more strange event at you.

A KING COMING ON A DONKEY

Zechariah 9:9 Rejoice greatly, O daughter of Zion; shout, O daughter of Jerusalem: behold, thy King cometh unto thee: he is just, and having salvation; lowly, and <u>riding upon an ass</u>, and upon a colt the foal of an ass.

Matthew 21:5 Tell ye the daughter of Sion, Behold, thy King cometh unto thee, meek, and <u>sitting upon an ass</u>, and a colt the foal of an ass.

Daniel 9:25-27 Know therefore and understand, that from the going forth of the commandment to restore and to build Jerusalem unto the Messiah the Prince shall be seven weeks, and threescore and two weeks: the street shall be built again, and the wall, even in troublous times. And after threescore and two weeks <u>shall Messiah be cut off</u>, but not for himself: and the people of the prince that shall come shall destroy the city and the sanctuary; and the end thereof shall be with a flood, and unto the end of the war desolations are determined. And he shall confirm the covenant with many for one week: and in the midst of the week he shall cause the sacrifice and the oblation to cease, and for the overspreading of abominations he shall make it desolate, even until the consummation, and that determined shall be poured upon the desolate.

The Scriptures above speak of Jesus coming to present Himself to Israel as their Messiah. It was foretold that He would ride in on a donkey in Zechariah 9:9. Jesus rode into Jerusalem on the 10th of Nisan which is the exact day the Jews were commanded in Exodus 12 to choose a lamb for Passover. This lamb would be killed on Passover the 14th of Nisan. Daniel 9:25-27 shows that the Jews would reject and kill (cut off) their Messiah. This happens at the end of the 69th week of years. It is worth noting that Matthew

Chapter 21-27 covers the last four days of the life of Christ. Jesus curses the fig tree in Matthew 21:19. *And when he saw a fig tree in the way, he came to it, and found nothing thereon, but leaves only, and said unto it, Let no fruit grow on thee henceforward for ever. And presently the fig tree withered away. (Matthew 21:19)*

This takes place on the 11th of Nisan, just three days before He goes to the cross. The fig tree seems to be figurative of the nation of Israel and shows the Lord's attitude towards them for their rejection of Him as their Messiah.

John 12:1-15 gives an account of the same story of Jesus riding in on the donkey and the timeline is easy to see there as verse 1 starts out with, *"six days before the Passover."* Jesus told His disciples to bring him a donkey that had never before been ridden. Christ rode this donkey from the mountain of Olives into the Kidron Valley below on the 10th of Nisan. Many of the Jews had gathered to meet Him there and placed palm branches in His path and sang *"Hosanna, blessed is the king of Israel that cometh in the name of the Lord."* Jesus then went into Jerusalem through the Eastern Gate. (You can see this on the front cover of the book) This gate is also referred to as the Golden Gate. The High Priest would be at the Temple choosing a lamb at this very moment, a lamb to be killed on Passover. He had no idea the true Lamb had already been chosen by God and had entered the city through the eastern Gate! Four days later many of the same Jews who shouted praises to Him would be in the crowd crying "crucify Him." There are eight gates that lead into the city of Jerusalem. The Eastern Gate was sealed up and the Ottoman Turks (Muslims) put a cemetery in front of it in the 1500's in hopes of keeping the Messiah from entering the city. I believe when Jesus comes back on the

Day of Atonement that He will stand upon the Mountain of Olives. He will then ride the white horse through the Kidron Valley and enter Jerusalem through this same eastern Gate just as He did 2000 years prior. I believe the saints will be with Him. The Bible makes it clear that Jesus is coming back to the earth just as He left. He left from the Mountain of Olives forty days after Calvary. I believe He returns to the very same spot. *Which also said, Ye men of Galilee, why stand ye gazing up into heaven? this same Jesus, which is taken up from you into heaven, shall so come in like manner as ye have seen him go into heaven. (Acts 1:11)*

Let's make sure we understand all this. It was prophesied in Daniel 9 that Messiah would present Himself to Israel at the end of the 69th week of years. That was 483 years after the command to rebuild and restore Jerusalem given by Cyrus the King of Persia in the book of Ezra. This prophesy in Daniel 9 was fulfilled on the 10th of Nisan, four days before Passover. The account as told in John 12 makes the date very clear. Jesus rode a donkey from the Mount of Olives and across the Kidron Valley on Palm Sunday the 10th of Nisan. The Jews put palm branches down and shouted praises. Jesus then rode in through the Eastern Gate and presented Himself as their Passover Lamb. He went to the Temple and threw out the moneychangers. The Jews rejected their Messiah and placed Him on a cross.

Now, with that in mind, note what the Bible says here: *John 5:43 I am come in my Father's name, and ye receive me not: if <u>another shall come</u> in his own name, him ye will receive.*

I believe this is a reference to Palm Sunday. I believe Jesus is speaking of the 10th of Nisan when He rides in to present Himself as the Messiah and King of Israel. He is foretelling His rejection. *John 1:11 He came unto his own,*

211

and his own received him not.

Then He says, *"if another shall come in his own name, him ye will receive."* I believe He is foretelling the time when the Jews accept the false Messiah, the Antichrist. You see, we are all awaiting a deliverer today. The Catholics are planning to bring in the Kingdom when the False Prophet, whom most believe will be the Pope, joins with Antichrist. The Muslims are awaiting the 12th Imam who is suppose to come up out of a well and rule for seven years. You and I, the saints, are awaiting the rapture where we will meet the Lord in the air and have a seven-year wedding feast. The Jews are also awaiting the coming of Messiah but they rejected the true Christ and are going to accept the false Messiah, the Antichrist. That is what the Lord meant in John 1:11 above, *"if another shall come in his own name, him ye will receive."*

The True Messiah presented Himself to Israel on Palm Sunday by riding into Jerusalem on a donkey. He did this in fulfillment of the prophecy in Daniel 9. Christ fulfilled it right to the exact day. God is always right on time which is why I personally believe the fall feasts will be fulfilled perfectly and right on time as well. Since Satan counterfeits all that God has, it is very possible that Satan will present his counterfeit Messiah to Israel in this same manner and on this same day, the 10th of Nisan. There is something very interesting that happened in March of 2013 that I want to share with you. In fact, it has to do with the President riding into Jerusalem on a donkey.

The President Coming on a Donkey

In February of 2013, the President announced he would make his first trip to Israel. Look at the following timeline of events in light of what we just discussed above. This information is absolutely shocking. I was reluctant to place this in the book for fear of being misunderstood, but how do you ignore something like this? I want to make it very clear to the reader that I am not saying President Obama is or is not the Antichrist. I do not believe any of us can be sure of the identity of the man of sin. He will not be revealed to the world until the church is gone. The Bible tells us there are many antichrists. In fact, there have been several men in history that had all the attributes of the Antichrist. I personally believe that Satan always has a man on the scene that he is preparing because even he does not know the time of the end. With that said, let me give you some stunning events that took place back in February and March of 2013.

1. Feb. 11, 2013: Pope Benedict XVI announces his resignation as Pope. This announcement is made just <u>six days</u> after President Obama made his itinerary known concerning his trip to Israel. The pope officially resigns <u>16 days</u> later on February 28th at 8 PM.
http://en.wikipedia.org/wiki/Resignation_of_Pope_Benedict_XVI

2. Feb. 11, 2013: <u>6 hours</u> after announcing he would resign, lightning strikes St Peters Basilica in Rome at <u>6 p.m.</u>
    Monday just hours after Pope Benedict XVI announced his resignation, according to the BBC. The lightning strike happened around 6 p.m. local time.
Huffington Post 02-12-13
http://www.huffingtonpost.com/2013/02/12/lightning-strikes-st-peters-basilica-rome-photo_n_2668850.html

This Scripture immediately comes to mind:
Luke 10:18 And he said unto them, I beheld Satan as lightning fall from heaven.

3. Pope Benedict XVI is the first Pope in <u>600 years</u> to resign. In fact he is said to be one of only <u>six Popes ever</u> to resign,

though this is hard to document through history.   Pope Benedict was the 112th Pope.   The 911 emergency call system in Italy is 112. Isn't that interesting? In Europe when they write the date they do not write it as 2-11-13 like we do here in America, they would write it 11-2-13.   The 112th Pope announced his resignation in 2013. Interesting isn't it? The 113th Pope began his reign on March 13, 2013 after being announced as the new Pope at 8:13 p.m.   But there is more: The new Pope was elected seven days before Obama arrives in Israel. Also worth noting is that the United States Federal Government declared all payments would be electronic by March 13, 2013. There will be no more checks from the Federal Government which is one more step towards the cashless society. This began the same day the 113th Pope took office, one week (7 days) before the President arrives in Israel on the 10th of Nisan.

The Treasury Department is phasing out paper checks and will move to a fully automated system by March 13, 2013. The move, announced today, is expected to save $1 billion over the next 10 years in Social Security costs and $120 million annually overall. http://gcn.com/Articles/2010/12/21/Federal-checks-go-all-electronic.aspx

4. 2000 years ago Christ made His appearance to Israel on Nisan 10, we call it Palm Sunday. President Obama arrived in Israel the afternoon of March 20th which is the Eve of Nisan 10. The 10th of Nisan began at 6:00 p.m. that very day. The 10th of Nisan began at sundown on March 20th, just a few hours after the arrival of Airforce One.

5. Most of President Obama's diplomacy took place on the 10th of Nisan.

February 12, 2013, YNet News –

Jerusalem and Washington have set the itinerary for President Barack Obama visit to Israel. Obama is scheduled to land in Ben Gurion International Airport around noon on Wednesday, March 20 (Nisan 9). He will be welcomed by a State reception which will include speeches by President Shimon Peres, Prime Minister Benjamin Netanyahu and by the American president himself.

Obama will then fly to Jerusalem directly to Peres' residence where he'll again be ceremoniously received. He will continue with Peres and Netanyahu to Yad Vashem Holocaust Museum, where he will lay a wreath in the Hall of Remembrance. The next stop will be Mount Herzl, where Obama will lay a wreath on Herzl's tomb as a gesture to Zionism. Obama will continue to Yitzhak Rabin's tomb, laying a wreath there as well. In the afternoon [of Nisan 9] the entourage will arrive at the prime minister's house, where Netanyahu and Obama will meet with small delegations to discuss issues such as Iran, Syria, the peace process and Jonathan Pollard. Following the meeting a joint press conference will be held, after which the two and their staff will dine together. (After sunset, Palm Sunday Nisan 10.)

http://www.ynetnews.com/articles/0,7340,L-4343916,00.html

6. Jesus came riding a donkey, Obama presented himself to Israel supported by the Democratic Party which has a donkey as its symbol.

7. Jesus was praised when He presented Himself to Israel. President Obama received honor and praise upon his arrival. There was even an ice sculpture, an "image" of President Obama made in his honor. (Revelation 13:14)

President Barack Obama will receive Israel's Presidential Medal of Distinction when he visits the Jewish state next month, making him the first sitting U.S. president to receive the honor.

The National Memo 02-18-2013

http://www.nationalmemo.com/obama-to-receive-presidential-medal-of-distinction-on-israel-trip/

They will also be taken to an Israel Museum's exhibition about King Herod and to the Ice city where they will see a custom built ice sculpture in Obama's image.

Ynet News 02-20-2013

http://www.ynetnews.com/articles/0,7340,L-4347338,00.html

8. Jesus entered Jerusalem as the Prince of Peace. Obama entered as a bearer of what's called an "unshakable alliance." I am sure we all understand that after the rapture the Antichrist will make a seven-year peace treaty with Israel. This is certainly interesting in light of that.

Israel has named Obama's visit "Unshakable Alliance." Translated compactly from the Hebrew words *brit amim*, or an alliance of nations, the phrase echoes variations on the theme repeated by U.S. leaders in recent decades, from Obama's "unshakable commitment" to Israel's security, to Hillary Rodham Clinton's "unshakable bond" and way back to Dan Quayle's "unshakable alliance."

Los Angeles Times Feb 18, 2013
http://articles.latimes.com/2013/feb/18/world/la-fg-wn-obama-visit-israel-logo-20130218

Quoting the 'Times of Israel' website: "Obama had indicated in the past that he would come to Israel only when he truly believed it would enable a breakthrough in Israeli-Palestinian relations.

www.timesofisrael.com/obama-to-visit-israel-within-weeks/

9. There was some confusion about the Lord's place of birth, just as there is great controversy about President Obama's place of birth. You see, prophesies in the Old Testament said Messiah would be from Bethlehem of Judea. *Micah 5:2 But thou, Bethlehem Ephratah, though thou be little among the thousands of Judah, yet out of thee shall he come forth unto me that is to be ruler in Israel; whose goings forth have been from of old, from everlasting.*

According to Luke Chapter 2 the Lord Jesus was born in Bethlehem exactly as Scripture said He would. Thirty years later, when He began His ministry, he came from Nazareth. This brought some confusion and doubts to some. *Philip findeth Nathanael, and saith unto him, We have found him, of whom Moses in the law, and the prophets, did write, Jesus of Nazareth, the son of Joseph. And Nathanael said unto him, Can there any good thing come out of Nazareth? Philip saith unto him, Come and see. John 1:45-46*

There are a lot of unanswered questions about the birth of Obama. If there is not anything to hide, you have to wonder why the President has spent over a million dollars on lawyers to hide his records. In fact, what do we really know about this man? He came out of nowhere and has never been required to show any documentation to anyone. It is very strange. His college records are a mystery. His Hawaiian birth records are a mystery. His whole life is a mystery. It is almost like he has no past at all. There has never been a friend, a classmate, or even an old girlfriend that has come forward and said they knew Mr. Obama from college days.

The GPS coordinates for Bethlehem where the true Messiah was born is as follows.

Decimal Minutes (GPS) : N31 42.34926 E35 12.15996

President Obama's father is said to have been born near the shores of Lake Victoria just outside Kendu Bay, Kenya. I am told that the GPS coordinates for this very place are nearly the same as Bethlehem except the decimal point is moved so that the top number reads N.31 instead of N31. If this is true, and I do not know that it is, it would be interesting. This whole trip to Israel on the 10th of Nisan is quite a coincidence, or is it?

What in the World is Going on?

Things are happening so fast around the world that you can hardly keep up with them. If it isn't a natural disaster it is a mass shooting or a terrorist threat. There are fresh scandals each and every week. We have the Benghazi scandal, the IRS scandal, the Obama-care debacle, and on and on we could go. America is polarized between conservatives and liberals. Financial bailouts and a huge national debt that is out of control have people on edge. It is just a matter of time and it is all going to crumble. This amazing news item about the debt came out while I am writing this chapter. How bizarre is that?

Debt Up $6.666 Trillion Under Obama

From CNS News dated February 4, 2014:

When President Obama was first inaugurated on Jan. 20, 2009, the debt of the U.S. government was $10,626,877,048,913.08, according to the Treasury Department's Bureau of the Public Debt. As of Jan. 31, 2014, the latest day reported, the debt was $17,293,019,654,983.61—an increase of $6,666,142,606,070.53 since Obama's first inauguration. The total debt of the United States did not exceed $6.666 trillion until July 2003. In the little more than five years of the Obama presidency, the U.S.

has accumulated as much new debt as it did in it's first 227 years.

http://cnsnews.com/news/article/ali-meyer/debt-6666-trillion-under-obama#nationaldebt

What does it all mean? What in the world is going on?

I believe the world is being prepared for three things.

1. The world is being prepared for the return of Jesus Christ.

2. The world is being prepared for the Kingdom of Antichrist.

3. The world is being prepared for God's final Jubilee.

In a nutshell, I just gave the reason for all the crazy things going on in the world in recent months and years. If we are near the end of the Church Age then some things have got to be in place. If the Antichrist is getting ready to be revealed, there must be a world kingdom in place for him to rule. If God's final Jubilee is getting ready to begin, the six-thousandth prophetic year must be near. Let's review these three statement:

1. The world is being prepared for the soon return of Jesus Christ.

Certain things have got to be in place when the Lord comes for His bride. The Lord will remove us from a lukewarm Laodicean Church described in Revelation 3. A large percentage of people within this church will be unsaved as we learned with the parable of the ten virgins. A global one-world church philosophy will be prevalent with a charismatic leader ready to emerge and bring all religions together to follow the Antichrist. Friend, this system is alive and well right now. That man may in fact have been put in place on 3-13-13 at 8:13 in Rome. The number "13" is the number associated with bad things for many people. The False Prophet is the religious leader of the one-world church that exists right before and after the rapture. He will point people to the false Messiah, the Antichrist. Most prophecy teachers agree that this man is the Pope and that he leads the one-world church. I have had Catholic people tell me the

218

same thing. What in the world is going on? The world is being prepared for the soon return of the Lord Jesus Christ.

2. The world is being prepared for the soon coming of Antichrist and his kingdom.

The Bible says that after we are gone the Antichrist becomes the one-world dictator.

And I saw when the Lamb opened one of the seals, and I heard, as it were the noise of thunder, one of the four beasts saying, Come and see. And I saw, and behold a white horse: and he that sat on him had a bow; and a crown was given unto him: and he went forth conquering, and to conquer. (Revelation 6:1-2)

Since this happens right after the rapture, we know the Antichrist must be a grown man and ready to take his place before the saints are taken out. The Antichrist will rule over the revived Roman Empire as prophesied in the book of Daniel. Let me give you a little review of this here.

Daniel 2, Daniel 7, and Revelation 13:1-2 are all basically the same story. They speak of four kingdoms in history that rule the whole world. Actually, there are five if you count the revived Roman Empire that arises during the Tribulation. There have only been four times in history since the Israelites crossed the Red Sea and left Egypt that the world has been under a one-world dictatorship. The four kingdoms were Babylon, Persia, Greece, and Rome. The fifth time shall be during the Tribulation, and will be the revived Roman Empire which is a renewal of the fourth empire. It will be made up of the ten European nations. (The ten toes & ten horns in Daniel 2&9) These are all in place and even have a common currency, the Euro dollar. Antichrist will head up this empire. Everything is ready for the Antichrist to rule the world. Only one thing is stopping him and that one thing is the church of God. In the chart below, I give the world empires, and how they are described in the Bible. As I said,

Daniel 2 and 7 and Revelation 13 all speak of the same four world kingdoms. Notice in Daniel 2 that Nebuchadnezzar saw the kingdoms of the world as metals in the form of a statue. He was the head of gold and of course, quite happy about it. That is how worldly man thinks, isn't it? They think in terms of value and wealth and power and might. However, the vision that Daniel saw in Chapter 7 tells of the same world empires, but God describes them as wild beasts. God sees things different than man sees things. God views the kingdoms of the world as wild beasts that can not be tamed. These wild beasts grow and eventually devour and destroy everything that does not submit to them. Each year the beast will need to be fed more than the year before. We can certainly see that here in America. With 17 trillion in debt and a Government that is growing faster than the private sector; bad things are in our future. In Daniel 2, the worldly king sees the kingdoms of the world as precious metals to be sought and as power and might to destroy its enemies. In Daniel 7, God shows the Prophet Daniel that the kingdoms of the world are wild beasts that can not and will not be tamed. Notice that Revelation 13 shows the kingdom of the Antichrist will have qualities from each of the four kingdoms of the past. John records them backwards in Revelation 13 because he is looking from future to the past. *And I stood upon the sand of the sea, and saw a beast rise up out of the sea, having seven heads and ten horns, and upon his horns ten crowns, and upon his heads the name of blasphemy. And the beast which I saw was like unto a leopard, and his feet were as the feet of a bear, and his mouth as the mouth of a lion: and the dragon gave him his power, and his seat, and great authority. And I saw one of his heads as it were wounded to death; and his deadly wound was healed: and all the world wondered after the beast. And they worshipped the dragon which gave power unto the beast: and they*

worshipped the beast, saying, Who is like unto the beast? who is able to make war with him? (Revelation 13:1-4)
Notice that Satan is also likened unto a wild beast, a dragon. He gives these kingdoms their power and the final kingdom has attributes of all four prior kingdoms. This final empire must be in place and ready to be ruled by him. A peace treaty is going to be signed between Israel and the Antichrist right after the rapture. Since that is the case, then obviously Israel has to be in their homeland and seeking peace. Therefore, this system must be in place before we are taken out at the rapture. "What in the world is going on?" God is preparing the world for the coming of the Antichrist and his kingdom. I believe that time is very near.

World Kingdoms Daniel Chapter 2, Daniel Chapter 7, Rev 13

World Kingdom	Daniel 2	Daniel 7	Revelation 13
1. Babylon Daniel's day 605 BC Nebuchadnezzar	Head of gold	Lion with eagle's wings	mouth of lion
2. Media-Persia 536 B.C.	Chest & arms of silver	Bear	Feet of Bear
3. Greece 322 B.C. Alexander the great!	Belly & Thigh of brass	Leopard four wings	Like Leopard
4. Rome 63 B.C.	Legs of iron	Dreadful beast	A Beast
5. Antichrist Revived Roman Empire	Feet of iron and clay (Ten toes)	Ten horns	Ten horns
6. Christ's Kingdom	Stone cut out without hands (Dan 2:34)	Everlasting kingdom (Dan 7:27)	

3. The world is being prepared for the arrival of God's final Jubilee.

All of us have important events scheduled from time to time. As those events get closer we tend to begin to prepare for them. For instance, my daughter just had her first baby a few weeks ago. She knew the baby was coming several months ago, and she and her husband began to prepare for it. They began buying things they would need. They bought a crib and a changing table and other items. It was not until after the eighth month that they began to have the suitcase packed and ready and made sure there was gas in the car in preparation for that day. You see, they knew for several months that a baby was coming, but the closer they got to the due date the more they prepared for it. I believe this same thing should be true for us concerning the coming of the Lord. I believe an understanding of the signs of the times and a realization that Christ is coming soon will bring about an urgency of God's people to get their lives in order.

But ye, brethren, are not in darkness, that that day should overtake you as a thief. (1 Thessalonians 5:4)

So likewise ye, when ye shall see all these things, know that it is near, even at the doors. (Matthew 24:33)

Not forsaking the assembling of ourselves together, as the manner of some is; but exhorting one another: and so much the more, as ye see the day approaching. (Hebrews 10:25)

There are some things that a person in Bible days would do in preparation for a coming Jubilee. If you had a big farm with several bond servants, you would have to be looking to hire some men because at the Jubilee all bond servants become free. They do not have to leave but if they choose to stay you will now have to pay a competitive wage. If you happen to be farming some land that you acquired from someone of another tribe, you will need to make some arrangements because that property is going back to the original owner at the Jubilee. You see, some planning needs to be done in advance of the Jubilee. The same is true of the Lord. As God's final Jubilee draws near, certain things have got to be in place. God is a God of order. God is always right on time. He is never early and He is never late. The Lord Jesus Christ is coming back to the earth on the Day of Atonement on the 70th Jubilee. He will have in His hand the title deed to this earth. Everything will be in order. Everything will be in place. Every prophecy will have been fulfilled and it will be the exact time of the exact month of the exact prophetic year for His return. What in the world is going on? The world is being prepared for God's final Jubilee. *Revelation 22:20 He which testifieth these things saith, Surely I come quickly. Amen. Even so, come, Lord Jesus.*

Will Antichrist Fulfill the Seven Feasts?

There are seven feasts in Leviticus 23 that we have talked about throughout this book. Jesus has fulfilled the first four right to the day. The final three are fall feasts and it is very possible that they too will be fulfilled right to the day. The Antichrist is a false Christ. He is coming to be the Messiah to Israel, but he is a false Messiah. Satan is a deceiver and has a counterfeit to everything God has. For instance, Satan deceives the world with false hopes and empty promises of joy and happiness in the liquor bottle or in fornication. He offers counterfeit homes by way of the "gay" or "swinger" lifestyle. He has a counterfeit church that will bloom before and after the rapture. It is in fact here even now. Just as God gave man the written word, Satan offers to the world his watered down corrupt versions of the Scriptures. God is a Trinity consisting of the Father, the Son and the Holy Spirit. Satan the counterfeiter will have his trinity: Satan, Antichrist and the false prophet. Antichrist is the false Christ, and the false prophet is the one-world religious leader representing the Holy Spirit. Have you ever wondered what the mark of the beast is all about? Let me give you something to think about concerning it. *And he causeth all, both small and great, rich and poor, free and bond, to receive <u>a mark</u> in their right hand, or in their foreheads: And that no man might buy or sell, save he that had <u>the mark</u>, or the name of the beast, or the number of his name. Here is wisdom. Let him that hath understanding count the number of the beast: <u>for it is the number of a man; and his number is Six hundred threescore and six</u>. (Revelation 13:16-18)*

Six is the number of man. Three is the number of divinity. Seven is the number of perfection. Six falls just short of perfection. Satan establishes his counterfeit trinity but it does not measure up to God's perfection. The three sixes represent Satan, Antichrist, and the false prophet. This trinity falls short of God but, like all cults, it has truth mixed with error to deceive people into accepting it. This false trinity of Satan will eventually control all commerce, banking, religion and government. **Accepting the "mark of the beast" will in fact be putting your trust in the Antichrist just as a believer today would place his trust in Jesus.** I hope that what I have just shared with you will help you understand better because there is a lot of misunderstanding concerning this today. The Antichrist comes on a white horse in Revelation 6:1-2 to save the world. It is simply a counterfeit of the true Christ returning on a white horse in Revelation 19:11-21.

With the great counterfeiter in mind, and since the seven feasts are such an important part of the whole order of prophetic things, is it possible that Antichrist will also fulfill his version of the seven feasts? Jesus certainly seems to have given us that impression in the following verse that we looked at earlier: *I am come in my Father's name, and ye receive me not: <u>if another shall come in his own name</u>, him ye will receive. (John 5:43)*

Let's have a look at some possibilities of how Satan could

fulfill the seven feasts.

1. Feast of Passover: Nisan 10 (Palm Sunday) Antichrist presents himself to Israel with a seven-year peace treaty in hand. 3 ½ years later on Passover the Antichrist enters the temple in Jerusalem (Abomination of Desolation, Matt. 24) and claims to be the Jewish Messiah.

2. Feast of Unleavened Bread: Jesus lay in the tomb during this time. The Antichrist could receive the deadly wound in fulfillment of this feast. (Revelation 13:3)

3. Feast of Firstfruits: Antichrist rises back to life and power just as Christ rose from the dead. (Rev 13:11-15)

4. Pentecost: Antichrist calls fire down from Heaven. It may be his fulfillment of Pentecost. (Revelation 13:13)

5. Feast of Trumpets: There is a rapture of the Tribulation saints that takes place at the Second Coming of Christ. The saved on the earth will join us.

6. Day of Atonement: Satan leads his armies to the battle at Armageddon just as Jesus leads His armies to the same battle. (Revelation 19)

7. Feast of Tabernacles: Satan is thrown into the bottomless pit for 1000 years. Jesus sets up the 1000 year Kingdom Age. It is very interesting that President Obama fulfilled Nisan 10 back in March of 2013. As I write this, he and Secretary of State John Kerry are working diligently to come up with a peace treaty in Israel. Whatever or whoever comes up with a peace deal, it will have to effectively take care of the Palestinian problem. I believe the rebuilding and approval of the 3rd Jewish Temple will also be a part of the peace process that is brokered with Israel. In fact, I believe it will be the "carrot" that makes the deal go through. I want to make it very clear that I am not saying that President Obama is the Antichrist. What I am saying is that whoever the Antichrist will be, he is very possibly going to fulfill the seven feasts because Satan counterfeits everything of God's.

Epilogue

We have discussed many important truths in this book. We have studied ten proofs of a Pre-Tribulation rapture. We have examined three ways to interpret Scripture. We have gone into great detail to shine the light on God's prophetic time-clock, the seven feasts. We have discovered that God's 70th Jubilee is on the near horizon and that we are very close to the end of the 6000th year of human history. We have concluded that we are very possibly the last generation to live before the coming of the Lord, which explains "what in the world is going on!"

Friend, what will you do with this information? Will you share these truths with others? Will you get on your knees and ask God to cleanse your heart and use you in these last days?

Most importantly, are you ready to meet the Lord? Are you a born again child of God, ready to meet Him?

If you are not 100% sure you are saved, I invite you to read the last few pages of this book that deal with being 100% certain of Heaven.

Surely the Lord GOD will do nothing, but he revealeth his secret unto his servants the prophets.
(Amos 3:7)

CAN A PERSON BE 100% CERTAIN OF HEAVEN

One of the most important questions in all the world for a person to answer, is how to know for certain about his eternal destiny. Can a person know for certain that he is going to Heaven? Let me answer that with a question if I may. Would a loving God leave us down here to wonder and worry about our eternal destiny? Would a loving God leave it to chance? No, my friend, God has not left us here to worry and fret about our eternal destiny. He has made a way for every person to be saved and to KNOW they are saved. 2 Peter 3:9 *The Lord is not slack concerning his promise, as some men count slackness; but is longsuffering to us-ward, not willing that any should perish, but that all should come to repentance.*

Let me say here that you CAN be 100% certain of going to Heaven when you die. I chuckle as I think of the young boy who was asked if a person can know He is going to Heaven. The lad replied, "Yes." "Well, how do you get to Heaven?" the critic asked again with a grin. To this the boy replied, "Well, sir, you first got to die." The boy had it partly right, you've got to die first, and the truth is we are all going to die and face God one day. (Maybe sooner than any of us thinks.) In this chapter I plan to show you from the Bible that a person CAN be 100% certain of Heaven when he dies, and what we must do to be certain. Ask yourself honestly, do you know 100% for certain that your destination is Heaven when you die? Is there a time or a place in your mind that you remember getting born again? Should God ask you why you deserve to be let into Heaven, would you have a Scriptural answer? Are you unsure as to your eternal destiny? Would you like to be 100% sure about Heaven? Do you wonder what a person must do to get to Heaven? Is it good deeds, church membership, baptism, reformation, or a combination of these? Can a person REALLY be 100% sure of Heaven before he dies? If you are not sure about Heaven, but are honestly searching for the truth, please read on as I not only show you from the Bible that one CAN be 100% sure of Heaven, but I will also show you how you can be 100% sure that Heaven is YOUR eternal destination today! You say, "You don't know me or what I have done." I don't care what you have done; Christ came to save sinners, little sinners, and big sinners. He saved that wicked thief and murderer who was crucified next to Him; He will save you, too, if you will do what the Bible requires for salvation.

As we begin to search the Scriptures together, ask the Lord to speak to you and show you the truth. Tell Him you want to spend eternity in Heaven, open your heart and mind and let God speak to you. Say something like this: "Dear God, I do not have the assurance of eternal life in Heaven. Please speak to my heart and help me to understand what your Word, the Bible, says about it so I can be saved and have 100% assurance of Heaven today, Amen."

I. FIVE MEN WHO WERE 100% SURE OF HEAVEN

1. KING DAVID KNEW WITH 100% CERTAINTY HE WAS GOING TO HEAVEN.

Then said his servants unto him, What thing is this that thou hast done? thou didst fast and weep for the child, while it was alive; but when the child was dead, thou didst rise and eat bread. And he said, While the child was yet alive, I fasted and wept: for I said, Who can tell whether GOD will be gracious to me, that the child may live? But now he is dead, wherefore should I fast? can I bring him back again? I shall go to him, but he shall not return to me. (2 Samuel 12:21-23)

I want you to see here that David had a child who was dying. For seven days he fasted and wept and prayed for the child to be healed, but the child died and went to Heaven as all babies do that die. Notice what David said in verse 23, "*I shall go to him, but he shall not return to me.*" You see, David had complete comfort and assurance that he would join his child in Heaven one day. He did not say that he hoped to see him, or he might see him, or he wanted to see him. He said, "I shall go to him." He had complete assurance that he was going to Heaven when he died.

2. THE APOSTLE PAUL KNEW WITH 100% CERTAINTY HE WAS GOING TO HEAVEN.

2 Timothy 4:6-8 For I am now ready to be offered, and the time of my departure is at hand. I have fought a good fight, I have finished my course, I have kept the faith: Henceforth there is laid up for me a crown of righteousness, which the Lord, the righteous judge, shall give me at that day: and not to me only, but unto all them also that love his appearing.

In the above text, Paul is getting ready to be put to death for his preaching of Christ, yet it is plain to see that Paul knew with 100% certainty that he was saved and on his way to Heaven. He said in 2 Corinthians 5:8 concerning saved folks, "*We are confident, I say, and willing rather to be absent from the body, and to be present with the*

Lord." Paul was absolutely sure about where believers go at death.

3. JOB KNEW WITH 100% CERTAINTY HE WAS GOING TO HEAVEN.

Job 19:25-27 For I know that my redeemer liveth, and that he shall stand at the latter day upon the earth: And though after my skin worms destroy this body, yet in my flesh shall I see God: Whom I shall see for myself, and mine eyes shall behold, and not another; though my reins be consumed within me.

Job knew his Redeemer was alive and well, and that he would see Him after he died.

4. PETER KNEW WITH 100% CERTAINTY HE WAS GOING TO HEAVEN.

Peter says in 1 Peter 1:4-5 *To an inheritance incorruptible, and undefiled, and that fadeth not away, reserved in heaven for you, Who are kept by the power of God through faith unto salvation ready to be revealed in the last time.*

You see, not only did Peter have assurance of Heaven, but he said, *"...reserved in heaven for YOU who are kept by the power of God..."* Talk about assurance, Peter is saying that we who have put our faith in Christ, not only have the assurance of Heaven, but that we are KEPT saved by God's power not ours! Now, friend, that is what you call being eternally secure!

5. JOHN KNEW WITH 100% CERTAINTY HE WAS GOING TO HEAVEN.

Read 1 John 5:13. *These things have I written unto you that believe on the name of the Son of God; that ye may know that ye have eternal life, and that ye may believe on the name of the Son of God.*

This is the man called John the Beloved. *"The apostle whom Jesus loved."* John wrote the Gospel of John, 1st, 2nd, and 3rd John, as well as the book of the Revelation. John knew with 100% certainty he had eternal life, and said that the Scriptures were given so that all believers can, *"Know that ye have eternal life."*

Now I have given you five of the many examples of men in the Bible who knew with 100% certainty that they were saved and going to Heaven when they died. These are folks just like us. *"God is no respecter of persons."* He does not love one more than another. Let me point out some things these men (as well as us today) all had in common.

229

II. WHAT THESE FIVE MEN HAD IN COMMON.

1. THESE FIVE MEN WERE SINNERS FROM BIRTH.

Romans 3:10 As it is written, There is none righteous, no, not one:
Romans 3:23 For all have sinned, and come short of the glory of God;
Romans 5:12 Wherefore, as by one man sin entered into the world, and death by sin; and so death passed upon all men, for that all have sinned....

You see, the Bible teaches that we are all born into this world with a serious problem. We are sinners, and sinners are condemned to suffer Hell for all eternity. You say, "I don't want to hear anything about hellfire and damnation." Well, go ahead and throw this book in the trash and listen to all the false teachers and liars out there then. As long as I have breath, I plan to tell people the honest truth of what the Bible teaches. There is a Hell that burns with fire for those who refuse to accept the plan of salvation which God has provided through Christ. This leads me to the second common trait I see in these five men:

2. THESE FIVE MEN WERE UNDER THE CONDEMNATION OF GOD AND DESTINED TO HELL.

Romans 6:23a "For the wages of sin is death..." And this death is the second death, the LAKE OF FIRE we read about in Revelation 20:14. *And death and hell were cast into the lake of fire. This is the second death."* And *Revelation 21:8 But the fearful, and unbelieving, and the abominable, and murderers, and whoremongers, and sorcerers, and idolaters, and all liars, shall have their part in the lake which burneth with fire and brimstone: which is the second death.* We read the chilling story of the rich man who died and went to Hell in Luke 16:23. *And in hell he lift up his eyes, being in torments, and seeth Abraham afar off, and Lazarus in his bosom.*

He did not go to Hell because he was rich; he went to Hell because he was not saved. There are scores of Scriptures we could look at concerning the truth of a literal, burning Hell. But that is in another chapter. What I want you to grasp is that these five men, as well as every other person born into this world, were sinners, and as such were under the judgment and wrath of God for their sin. John 3:18 *He that believeth on him is not condemned: but he that believeth not is condemned already, because he hath not believed in the name of the only begotten Son of God.* Every person will die and go to Hell unless he is cleansed in the blood of Jesus Christ. See 1 Peter 1:19.

3. THESE FIVE MEN WERE SINNERS NOT ONLY BY BIRTH, BUT IN THEIR PERSONAL LIVES AS WELL.

Listen, all five of these men were not only born in sin, (Psalm 51:5) but all five of them have many of their personal faults and mistakes and sins recorded in the Bible for all to see. How would you like for God to record some things concerning your past that nobody but you and God know about? If you do not get saved, your sins will be made known to all when the *"Books are Open"* at the Great White Throne judgment in Revelation 20:12-15. Let me give you just a few examples of the sins of some of these five men as recorded in God's Word:

PETER forsook the Lord and fled when Christ was betrayed in the garden. Later he denied he knew Christ and even cursed and swore. DAVID, the *man after God's own heart*, committed adultery with another man's wife, and had her husband, Uriah, killed to try and hide his sin. JOB was chastened by God for his lack of faith and understanding. PAUL was killing Christians before he got saved, and took a Jewish vow that was not biblical after he got saved, shaved his head, and went to Jerusalem after the Holy Spirit warned him not to go. Paul, when testifying of himself, stated that he was *"The Chief of Sinners."* Even JOHN the Beloved forsook Jesus, struggled with doubt, and quit the ministry for a while. You see, these men were not only born sinners, but they sinned throughout their lives just as you and I were born sinners, and you and I have sinned throughout our lives. If you are honest, you know this to be true. We have sinned against a holy God, we are under the condemnation of God, and must pay the penalty of death and Hell for it. But thanks be to God, He made a way for us to escape the judgment of Hell. This leads me to my final common attribute of these five men:

4. THESE FIVE MEN AT SOME POINT IN THEIR LIVES, ALL PUT THEIR FAITH AND TRUST IN CHRIST TO SAVE THEM.

You see, whether you live in the Old Testament, or the New Testament, or during the Great Tribulation to come, salvation is the same. It is through faith and trust in the finished work of Calvary! Salvation is by trusting what Jesus did on the cross as payment for sin. I don't want to take a lot of time to discuss the meaning of Bible dispensations here, but I do want to make plain to you that there is only one way to Heaven throughout the whole Bible, and that way is the cross of Christ! Salvation is through belief and trust in Christ. Many years before Christ, way back in Genesis, *Noah found grace in the eyes of the Lord*, Noah did not go to Heaven because he was good; he went by trusting in the grace of God who provided a Saviour for him. Abraham believed and trusted the Gospel according to Romans 4:1-5 *What shall we say then that Abraham*

231

our father, as pertaining to the flesh, hath found? For if Abraham were justified by works, he hath whereof to glory; but not before God. For what saith the scripture? Abraham believed God, and it was counted unto him for righteousness. Now to him that worketh is the reward not reckoned of grace, but of debt. But to him that worketh not, but believeth on him that justifieth the ungodly, his faith is counted for righteousness.

The Bible tells us that the Gospel was preached to the Old Testament people as well as unto us.

Hebrews 4:2 *For unto us was the gospel preached, as well as unto them: but the word preached did not profit them, not being mixed with faith in them that heard it.*

See, they needed faith in the Gospel of Christ to be saved just as we do. There were many Old Testament types that pointed to Christ. The "brazen serpent" of Numbers 21:9 which Jesus said in John 3:14 represented the cross. The Sabbath, the lamb's blood on the door post, the coats of skins for Adam and Eve, and on and on I could go. But these things did not save anyone nor did the keeping of the Law according to Hebrews 10:1-6, but rather were types to help the people understand and believe the Gospel. This is true of our New Testament baptism and communion ordinances. They do not save anyone, but are simply pictures and types of Christ and the Gospel. The Bible calls it *"The Everlasting Gospel"* in Revelation 14:6. You see, in the Old Testament, people had to trust in the coming Christ to save them. That is what the animal sacrifices and lambs represented or pictured. They had to place their faith in the coming Lamb of God and His personal sacrifice to save them. That is what John the Baptist meant concerning Jesus when he cried out, *"Behold the lamb of God which taketh away the sin of the world."* Jesus, the Messiah that all the lambs pictured, had arrived. It is no different looking forward to Calvary, than it is for us to look back to Calvary. Abraham had placed his faith in the coming Messiah to save him from his sins, just as Peter, Paul, and every other saved person in the New Testament must place their faith in the Christ who has already gone to the cross and paid the sin debt for us.

III. WHAT THESE FIVE MEN ARE SAYING TO YOU AND ME

1. We are all sinners, both from birth, and by our sinful lives.
Psalm 51:5 Behold, I was shapen in iniquity; and in sin did my mother conceive me.

232

Romans 3:10 As it is written, There is none righteous, no, not one:
Romans 3:23 For all have sinned, and come short of the glory of God;

2. We are all destined to Hell, the Lake of Fire, the second death, if we die in our lost and sinful condition.

Romans 6:23 "...the wages of sin is death..."

Revelation 20:15 And whosoever was not found written in the book of life was, cast into the lake of fire.

Revelation 21:8 But the fearful and unbelieving, and the abominable, and murderers, and whoremongers, and sorcerers, and idolaters, and all liars, shall have their part in the lake which burneth with fire and brimstone: which is the second death.

Do you see your condition before God? Do you realize that you are guilty before God and that as a sinner, God cannot let you into Heaven? Do you realize that sin must be paid for, and that God sent His own Son to pay for YOUR sin on the cross of Calvary?

John 3:16 For God so loved the world, that he gave his only begotten Son, that whosoever believeth in him should not perish, but have everlasting life.

Do you realize that if you do not choose to trust what Christ did on the cross as payment for your sin that you are choosing to go to Hell and pay on your sin debt for all of eternity?

3. Just as each of these five men made a personal choice, even so you must make a personal choice to trust in Christ to save you from Hell. You must realize that you are lost in your sin and destined for Hell. You must by faith, personally trust Jesus as your sin bearer, and fully trust Him as your personal Saviour. It is a simple act of faith that merits the grace of God.

Ephesians 2:8 For by grace are ye saved through faith; and that not of yourselves: it is the gift of God:
9 Not of works, lest any man should boast.

You must realize that your good deeds, your good life, or your membership at a church are not the way to Heaven. Those are good works. You must realize that the sacraments, or baptism, or any other good deed can never get your sins washed away. It is trusting by faith in the price that Jesus paid in full on Calvary that saves us, and that is what gives us 100% certainty of Heaven. Do you understand it? When that wicked jailer in Acts 16 asked Paul how to be saved, Paul told him to believe on the Lord Jesus Christ and put his faith in what Christ had done for him. Not just believe in Him, but on Him, as in trusting in. Look at what it says.

Acts 16:30. *And brought them out, and said, Sirs, what must I do to be saved?*
31 And they said, Believe on the Lord Jesus Christ, and thou shalt be saved, and thy house.

Friend, this man was saved by putting his faith and trust in Jesus. Paul did not give him a list of things to do, or tell the man to quit all his evil deeds, or join some church. He told him to put his faith and trust in Jesus Christ to be saved. Do you see it? Isn't that simple and right from the Word of God? So many theologians and religions have muddied the waters of the Gospel with tradition and opinions! Would you like to be saved? Simply bow your head right now wherever you are. Tell the Lord that you are a rotten sinner and undeserving of His love. Tell Him you believe Jesus is the Son of God, and you believe He died on the cross and paid the awful debt of sin that you owe, your eternal Hell. Tell Him that you believe He rose from the dead the third day, and by faith, you are right now repenting of your reliance on a church, or baptism, or some man, or good deeds, or sacrament, and are right now trusting the price Jesus paid on Calvary to save you from your sin, and from Hell, and to take you to Heaven when you die. AMEN!

Reciting a prayer will not save you, but if you have sincerely placed your faith and trust in Jesus Christ to save you, you can now say with 100% certainty that you know you are going to Heaven when you die. Praise the Lord and glory to His name.

Please contact me if you have trusted Christ as a result of reading this that I may rejoice with you. I also would like to send you some free information that will help you in your new life in Christ.

MORE FROM GOODWIN PUBLICATIONS
www.heavenboundone.net

Revelation Study Guide

Seven-Fold Promise

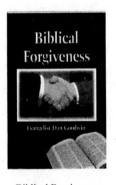

Biblical Forgiveness

Evangelist Dan Goodwin has written several other books and study guides that may be of help to you. Most are available in PDF for immediate download via e-mail.

Evangelist Dan Goodwin
80 Huff Lane
Reynolds Station, KY 42368
814-599-6280 (Text or call)
dgoodwin@uplink.net
www.heavenboundone.net

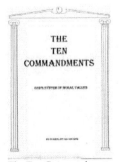

The Ten Commandments

Prophecy Conferences

Evangelist Dan Goodwin travels extensively, speaking in Prophecy Meetings and Bible Conferences across the nation. He has authored several books and study guides. Contact him to schedule a meeting or to get information on his books.

PROPHECY CONFERENCE TOPICS
* Are we the last generation
* Signs of the times
* What year is it anyway
* The seven feasts: God's Prophetic Calendar
* A wedding made in Heaven
* Solid proof of a pre-tribulation rapture
* God's final Jubilee
* The blood red moons
* The seven feasts and the Christian life
* The seven sealed book
* A 7000 year prophetic view
* Prophetic figures and types
* 2520

Evangelist Dan Goodwin
80 Huff Lane
Reynolds Station, KY 42368
814-599-6280 (Text or call)
dgoodwin@uplink.net
www.heavenboundone.net